*S*pirited
*W*omen

Spirited Women

Encountering the first women believers

Mary Ellen Ashcroft

Augsburg

MINNEAPOLIS

SPIRITED WOMEN
Encountering the First Women Believers

Cover painting copyright © 2000 Art Resource. Used by permission.
Cover design by Michelle L. Norstad
Book design by Timothy W. Larson

ISBN 0-8066-4027-8

Manufactured in the U.S.A.   AF 9-4027

04   03   02   01   00   1   2   3   4   5   6   7   8   9   10

For My Wonderfully Spirited Daughter, Susannah

LOOK TO THE ROCK from which you were hewn, and to the quarry from which you were dug. Look to Abraham your father and to Sarah who bore you.

— Isaiah 51:1-2

ALL THESE were constantly devoting themselves to prayer, together with certain women, including Mary, the mother of Jesus, as well as his brothers. . . . When the day of Pentecost had come, they were all together in one place. And suddenly from heaven there came a sound like the rush of a violent wind, and it filled the entire house where they were sitting.

— Acts 1:14—2:1

WHEN YOU COME TOGETHER, each of you has a hymn, a lesson, a revelation, a tongue, or an interpretation.

— 1 Corinthians 14:26

Contents

✤

Preface

❧

S PIRITED WOMEN IS AN INVITATION: an invitation to travel across time and space. It is an invitation to discover lost relatives in the faith.

Spirited Women can be read in a number of ways. It tells the story of the women who were present in the Gospels—last at the cross and first at the tomb—during the earliest years of the church. Many people who read *The Magdalene Gospel* asked me, "Well, then what? What happened to them after the Good Friday, Holy Saturday experience? Why do they seem to disappear?" *Spirited Women* is my way of answering that question based on research, intense biblical study, and imagination.

Spirited Women can also be read as a story of those early years about which individuals who have gone to church and read their Bibles for years often know little. I've set the story at a key moment in the life of the earliest church, when the Hellenistic believers are scattered after the death of Stephen—when they start to take the story on the road. Through these women's stories, individual and collective, I try to flesh out some of the challenges of those early days when many issues were being hammered out—pivotal areas like how much of Judaism to keep or throw out, how flexible to be in relation to local cultures, what being a believer in Jesus really meant. These were extraordinary times in the life of the church.

Others will want to read *Spirited Women* as a launching pad to deeper research into women's lives in the first-century Greco-Roman world, especially in the very early church. There is no shortage of material available on these topics, but much of it is scattered throughout learned texts, often in prose that is more scholarly than readable. To read *Spirited Women* in this way involves not only reading the material within the chapters but also consulting the notes for further reading at the back of the book (material with accompanying notes denoted by "see notes").

I also believe in the power of the scriptures to touch our lives today. To facilitate this, I have included chapter-by-chapter questions for individual readers who wish to allow their lives to interact with the lives of these, our spiritual foremothers. At this level, it is my hope that *Spirited Women* might provide an encounter with these women, allowing them to encourage and challenge us as contemporary women.

The women in *Spirited Women* (and in *The Magdalene Gospel*) met Jesus as individuals but also met Christ in each other and in the gathered community. Reflecting that, I have provided questions for group study and discussion, coming out of the individual questions, so that *Spirited Women* could provide a gathering point for a number of study sessions. I hope that many different kinds of women might be drawn into studying and discussing *Spirited Women*—those who are fully involved in the faith but who want to learn more about their foremothers, and those who have felt disenfranchised by the church and would like to engage in some honest discussion about Jesus, his relationship with women, and the way the church has treated women. I would hope that even those who are not at all sure about Jesus or the church might find *Spirited Women* to be a starting place. A number of people who work with Graduate Christian Fellowship have told me that they wanted to start a group for graduate students at their universities to study a Gospel, but that people felt so distanced from Scripture that they couldn't get them to join, and so they used *The Magdalene Gospel*, which offered a certain fictional distance. I hope that *Spirited Women* will function in the same way.

Finally, in a book like *Spirited Women*, the individual women's stories can function on their own. Many have used the stories from *The Magdalene Gospel* as parts of sermons, talks, and retreats. I would like *Spirited Women* to help similarly to bring from oblivion these voices unheard for too long.

People often express concern that writing about women's issues in the earliest church might lead to a sort of anti-Semitism, giving an impression that patriarchal Judaism was overthrown by a non-patriarchal Jesus and Christianity. *Spirited Women* is about the church figuring out what it meant to follow Jesus within patriarchal Jewish and Greco-Roman societies, which were pretty much equally (though not identically) oppressive. The overwhelming patriarchy of the church, after the short window of time written about here, should provide adequate proof that Christianity is as capable as any other faith or culture of being oppressive. If we believe that Jesus most fully reveals God's heart to humankind, however, then it makes sense that he stands out as a radical, remarkable embodied statement against the oppression prevalent in almost all organized religion.

I am grateful to many people for encouragement in writing *Spirited Women,* especially some spirited women who helped me work on this material in retreats and dramatic forms—Judy LeWin, Bette Schelper, Letha Wilson Barnard, Persis Elkins, Barb Olson, Kathy Langley, Kathy Nevins, Judy Hornbacher, Elizabeth Carlson, and Peg Birk.

Prologue

❧

IT WAS IN THE VATICAN MUSEUM that Bea turned to me. "You were lying to me yesterday when you said Jesus called women to follow him . . . that they were strong women. . . ."

We were in Rome together, Bea and I. The day before, we had walked eight hours, maybe more, visiting the Catacombs and the prison where Paul was chained. My heart was full as I walked in Rome that day.

I felt myself walking with those early believers, some wellborn, some prostitutes or slaves. Separated by almost two thousand years, we were connected by a common faith in Jesus, who had turned the known world upside down with his message of love, his strong voice against the hatred of women, his turning over of the religious establishment's tables. I told Bea how Jesus had called women to follow, had taught them, had befriended them, had touched them like no rabbi had ever done before. Women responded, and they were last at the cross and first witnesses to the resurrection. I told her how contemporaries derided the early Christian church as a movement of women, slaves, and children, because it was so radical in its day.

I imagined moving through the crowded streets with one who had just heard the good news, perhaps a slave, who on joining the new movement would have found herself treated as an equal for the first time in her life. Her womanhood, her slavery, would not have kept her on the fringes. She might have become a leader in the church, teaching, presiding at the eucharist. Time was nothing but a false veil that day: I walked where she'd walked.

At the Colosseum, I told Bea about Felicitas and Perpetua, who chose death over denying their beloved teacher; Perpetua had even handed over her baby so that she could be true to Jesus. After a day of walking, Bea and I slept well in our little pension.

The next day dawned wet and rainy: the perfect day to visit St. Peter's and the Vatican Museums.

Who is not stunned on entering St. Peter's, with its lines on the floor marking where smaller, insignificant European cathedrals would fit within its bulk? Bea and I joined groups of Japanese and German tourists milling around St. Peter's echoing marble and gilt spaces, gawking at its paintings and sculptures. The Christian movement was one of primitive paintings on cave walls, meetings in homes or catacombs, its tattered followers chained in prisons: these images seemed to fade in the hard marble reality of St. Peter's. Here was Christendom in all its glory, weight, and chill. Suddenly it hit me. Where were the women?

I spotted a few . . . crouched in the bottom right-hand corners of paintings, looking way, way up at slickly dressed patrons of the church, at St. Peter, at Jesus, at God. The Blessed Virgin stands everywhere, appearing as the church has dehumanized her in holy places—ever virgin, demure, available, looking downward, ever downward—a meek container for God.

We walked in the rain from St. Peter's to the Vatican Museum, hardly speaking as we got tickets and joined the crowds gawking at the massed art objects, making our way toward the Sistine Chapel.

Sculptures and paintings were layered high on the walls, one room after another, and in side galleries off to the left and right. Well-dressed men wielded power in their crimson robes, their gentrified finery: "this is the church" intoned ad nauseam. Thousands of pictures, hundreds of sculptures, and there are no women who resemble the ones in that early movement—strong, decisive, committed to following their radical teacher. The disjuncture between these art objects and the early movement was so gross, I could feel my face burning with anger. Honor wealth, lord it over the poor, banish women from real belonging: that's what the church stands for. With heavy hearts, we slipped into the Sistine Chapel and looked at God. And then Bea said it: "You were lying. . . ."

From that moment, I knew that this was a story that must be told. "Let's go find some lunch," I said, as we moved into the rainy afternoon. The disjuncture between the early movement and what we'd seen here gaps light years wide.

If the chasm was just in art, we could count it as the efforts of a church deeply twisted by a sexist society to justify its exclusion of women. But the gap seems to be everywhere—in Protestant churches where women have been barred from pulpits, in Catholic and Orthodox churches where they've been kept from celebrating the eucharist.

But the women seem to be missing, at least at first glance, in the New Testament. If I said to Bea: "Read the New Testament, and tell me where you see the women," she would find them in the Gospels, briefly in the book of Acts, and then in the last few verses of greetings in various epistles. It seems that scriptures themselves and the traditions of the Protestant, Catholic, and Orthodox branches of the church have all been complicit in centuries of marginalizing women.

"Where were they?" Bea demanded as the waiter brought salad. "Yesterday you told me about these incredible women and this radical guy, Jesus. Even if they were in the Gospels, like you wrote about in *The Magdalene Gospel*, they have been utterly, irretrievably lost. It seems like God is an old man, and Jesus—well, like father, like son. The Christian movement is for nicely dressed, disgruntled-looking men, throwing their weight around . . . walking over outsiders. Don't give me your damned wishful thinking, your fiction based on what you think should have happened, your revisionist take on the early church."

The Facts

Where are those lost women—our foremothers in the faith, the ones who followed Jesus in his earthly ministry, who were active leaders in the early church? Did they disappear except for a few folklore traces, like Mary Magdalene's finger that mysteriously turned up as a relic in Vezeley, or all the paintings of the blessed virgin Mary crowned queen of heaven? Is that all we have to go on—tracings of relics and mythical tales?

In fact, there is a surprising amount of factual information on women in the very early church that I could have rattled off to Bea in that little restaurant in Rome (see notes, 89). I might have told her that women were the first, the official witnesses to the resurrection, voicing the traditional apostolic announcement: "I have seen the Lord." Women were partners in the new missionary movement and played a major role in the house churches; Mary, mother of John (also called Mark), led a house group in Jerusalem, and these fellowships were true communities of equals, standing out against the predominant cultures of the time. Women were leaders in many of the earliest churches; the church at Philippi had three women as leading figures. Paul speaks highly of Priscilla (Prisca), mentioning her before her husband, speaking of her teaching skills, and saying that she risked her life for him. Women were given ministries through the laying on of hands, which had rabbinical "ordination" overtones.

The early church was such a friend to women that pagan writers like Celsus scoffed at Christianity for being a religion of women and slaves, because women held places of great responsibility in the church. On their conversions, women found themselves having to adjust from a patriarchal culture to one that was not. While male converts often gave up privileges when they became Christians, women who joined the new movement found themselves liberated, experiencing greater freedom of expression, education, and leadership than in society as a whole. Those who were slaves, foreign, poor, or working found places in the church. While the main function of women in both Jewish and Greco-Roman society was childbearing and rearing, in the new faith, women experienced a greater freedom to choose whether to be dependent on a man in marriage and whether to have children. Christianity intruded on patriarchal cultures in both Hellenistic and Jewish society, and Christianity was known as a way that women overcame dependency, as women were encouraged to move outside a narrow focus on the family.

The Story

I could have piled all this research on Bea, and it would have been factually true. But the depth of this troubling chasm that yawns between two millennia of the church's attitude toward women and Jesus' radical treatment of them is such that facts can hardly bridge it.

We need more than facts: we need flesh and blood; we need stories. And so, what I offer Bea and women like her is a kind of midrash, following a common practice in the first centuries after Christ, when Jewish writers used midrash to interpret the sacred writings known to us as the Old Testament (see notes, 92). Midrash, be it oral or written, uses as its springboard "a fixed, canonical text, considered the revealed word of God," and it is meant to bring God's word to an audience in a fresh way by holding two truths together—the authority of scripture and the "freedom of interpretation implicit in the conviction that Scripture speaks now, not only then." Midrash demands balance between these two, as the midrashist seeks to be faithful to the original and yet to mediate it to contemporary hearers. In this balance, midrash holds together what Jacob Neusner calls a "profoundly conservative and constructive power . . . while preserving the vitality and ongoing pertinence of revelation in the present age." To practice midrash, to try to balance these two, I base my stories on the biblical texts as well as on extensive research. Because of the lack of familiarity with this early period, I have provided much background on these women, both on their contemporary situations and on the way that they have been hidden by the church. But I believe that the real power is in the stories themselves.

To answer Bea and the many women who believe that the faith has marginalized them, to bring these foremothers (largely forgotten and silenced) to life for contemporary Christian women, I offer the story of these spirited women.

I believe in the communion of the saints and the life everlasting, and so I pull back the veil of time and space that has hidden these women from us for nearly two thousand years. By faith, by research, and by imagination, I sit with them at this table that stretches back, from now to then, from here to there. I pull back the veil and allow them to tell their stories while we listen.

Join me as we find our places at this table—we who are women at the beginning of a new millennium, sitting with our foremothers of the faith. As we begin, we might ask them: have you been lost, or have we? You have sat, watching these many years, waiting to welcome us. Perhaps it is in finding you that we find ourselves and our place in the faith.

One

Lost and Found at the Table

❧

Together at the Table

"THIS IS MY BODY," says Martha, slowly pulling apart a loaf of bread in front of her. "Jesus gave himself to us, for us," she adds, looking around the table at the women gathered, these followers of Jesus in the earliest church (see notes, 92).

These mothers of the church have gathered in Martha and Maria's Bethany home. "Each has a hymn, a lesson, a revelation" (1 Corinthians 14:26), as was the practice in these early days. Martha celebrates, Maria brings her experience of the Spirit and her visions of the church, Mary Magdalene tells of meeting the newly risen Jesus, and Suheir of deeply drinking the living water. Mary, mother of Jesus, speaks of a collaborative God, and Joanna of the struggle to follow in a divided church. Each brings her words and herself.

"Jesus gave himself for us, to us. . . . When I close my eyes, I still see him, dying," Maria, sister of Martha, says.

"Yes," says Mary Magdalene. "And yet he is alive."

"He is here, now," Joanna says. "The Spirit means he is always walking with us. He was there, dying . . . here in bread . . . with us, closer than close."

"With us and all the believers," adds Martha. They know believers are gathered all over the holy city, in Galilee, and beyond, because this is the first day of the week, when all meet to celebrate Jesus' resurrection.

"It is wonderful to be with you, to be here again," whispers Mary Magdalene. All these women live in Jerusalem, but they only see each other occasionally since the gift of the Spirit. Martha and Maria opened their Bethany home to this meeting, but most of its members are Aramaic-speaking believers. Mary, mother of Jesus, often comes, but Mary Magdalene and Joanna worship and minister in the Greek-speaking quarter of Jerusalem. Susannah has been staying here at Bethany with Martha and Maria, where she can speak her native Aramaic, but she has missed Mary Magdalene terribly. She sits with her arm entwined with Mary's, watching her face as she speaks.

As they pass the loaf, the women speak, sharing their lives as they share the meal. All is sacred while they are together.

"He is here, as you say, Mary," Mary, Jesus' says. "And yet you've come with some some great heaviness in your heart."

"Heavy, yes . . . very heavy," Mary Magdalene replies. "But not as heavy as it's been in this room before." She smiles at the faces around this table: these women have been through hell and heaven together. The mother of Jesus, Martha, Maria, Susannah, Mary Magdalene, and Joanna have sat in this room with hearts torn apart by sorrow and hearts overflowing with joy. Together they faced the death of their teacher. Together they heard the news of his resurrection. They met Jesus here, before and after his death; together they received the Spirit at Pentecost and have thrown themselves into the struggles of the infant church. Even now, as they look around the room, they feel the gaps left by Rhoda and Lydia, who have moved back to Galilee to work in house churches there, and Salome, whose anger threatens her faith. And there is another woman here, a foreigner, a Samaritan.

She hesitates when the bread comes to her, and Martha smiles and nods. She takes a chunk and eats it. "When I heard he was dead . . . and then Philip said, no, he was alive . . . but I needed to come and see and hear for myself. He changed my life. . . ."

"Jesus loves us so much," says Susannah as she takes the bread. "And yes, Mary, he is here." Susannah hands the bread to Mary Magdalene. "What is on your heart, child?"

Mary Magdalene puts the bread on the table in front of her. "We've decided to leave the holy city."

"We begin our journey tomorrow. For Antioch," Joanna tells them. "We'll go through Galilee and see some of the sisters there. We're traveling with Barnabas."

Tears spill down Susannah's cheeks. Mary holds her hand. "I'll never see you again . . ." the older woman weeps.

"It's Stephen, isn't it?" Mary, mother of Jesus, asks. "If anyone ever seemed to hold the Spirit, it was he" (see notes, 93).

"So young, and it did seem as if Jesus could have looked after him better," says Martha. "It's been very traumatic, especially to the Greek-speaking believers. Many are leaving the holy city. . . ."

"It's the scattering, the scattering . . ." Maria whispers.

All the women look at her.

"She's been seeing pictures—visions—and this is one," Martha explains. They wait, and Maria shakes her head. "Later."

"Right up to the end—when he was looking up and saw Jesus— I was sure he'd be rescued," Mary Magdalene says. "I guess we had no idea this could happen, with everything so new . . . the Spirit so real."

"Stephen's death changes everything," says Joanna. "We don't just spread the message, and then Jesus comes back. Suddenly, it's more complicated. That's why we came tonight. We want your prayers and blessings as we go."

Susannah wipes her eyes. Martha tells her, "Susannah, you know we will look after you."

"Susannah's exhausted, Mary. She hasn't told you that she spent the last few days with a charming young visitor, a Greek-speaking fellow named Luke who wanted eyewitness accounts—of Jesus' ministry, healings, words. His Aramaic was not bad . . . and her Greek isn't great, but they got along fine . . . didn't you, dear?" (see notes, 94).

"Yes, a fine young man, a new believer. Just as well he missed Salome," Susannah says, smiling. "She would have told him a thing or two."

"Yes, poor dear," Martha tells Joanna. "You haven't seen her, and so you wouldn't know that she was so distraught by Stephen's death. She felt that Stephen understood the message—all Jesus did and showed us—better than the leaders, especially James. She was set to tell James that he didn't really care about the heart of the faith, that he was no different from poor Ananias and Sapphira, who wanted to look good. . . .

"I suggested she go and stay with Lydia and Rhoda in Galilee. Rumor has it the believers there are a bit more radical than us Jerusalem folk. . . . They own only a few possessions in common, and other believers are family . . . seemed it might be just the thing for Salome."

"We'll visit her on our way," Joanna promises.

Susannah speaks again. "I just remembered something the young Greek said. He'd heard a rumor from Damascus, seems a bit farfetched, but that hothead Saul has met Jesus. You never know. . . ."

"Saul? He was there when Stephen died, looking like the picture of smugness. . . ." Mary Magdalene shakes her head. "I guess anything could happen."

"And Simon Peter," Joanna asks. "We haven't seen him for ages. How is he?"

"In a bit of a muddle, I'd say," says Martha. "He sympathizes with the believers who worship every day at the temple and see Jesus as the Messiah. But he was intrigued by Stephen's teaching. . . . I think he could see how the Spirit might supersede the law. In Peter's life, the Spirit has been utterly transforming. And now with Stephen's death, I think he's feeling very much on the fence."

"It's easy to forget what Peter was like before the gift," says Susannah. "He speaks so strongly, defying the authorities, wise to the leaders. And yet, sometimes it's hard for him . . . he feels so responsible. . . ."

Joanna shakes her head. "It's only going to get more complicated. The scattered believers are going to synagogues in other towns and telling proselytes and God-fearers about Jesus. Seems like Philip and the others went straight to places that would provoke the Aramaic-speaking believers—like Samaria" (see notes, 94).

"People have been coming in from the countryside to hear the word and to find healing," Martha says. "Who knows? Maybe God is doing a whole new thing . . . welcoming not only women and tax collectors and sinners, but taking the message to people who are not even members of the chosen." She looks at Mary Magdalene and Joanna. "Maybe you are part of a whole new . . . outside the holy city . . . you are witnesses. . . ."

Maria nods, "Yes, it all fits, yes. . . ."

"Pardon me for saying so," the Samaritan woman breaks in. "This is not new. When he spoke to me, Jesus told me we didn't need holy mountains or Jerusalem . . . that true worshipers would worship in spirit and truth."

"Spirit and truth," Maria says, nodding.

"And he was pleased when I took his message to others in my village. What you are talking about . . . the message going beyond, the message being too big for old structures, he told me . . . several years ago."

"True worshipers must worship in spirit and truth. . . . I like that; . . . those are Jesus words I'd never heard before," Joanna and the other women sit quietly and ponder (see notes, 95).

"It's those new wineskins again," says Joanna. The woman inclines her head.

"One of our favorite Jesus sayings. 'You can't put new wine in old wineskins, or they will burst. No, you need new skins for the new wine.' That's what he said, and we know it to be true. He did that for us in our lives."

"That's why you are going to Antioch," Maria says. "The new wine of the Spirit is not fitting the old wineskins. Just like he said."

Mary Magdalene picks up the bread and tears some off. She passes it to Maria, who also eats and hands it to Martha. Martha puts the bread on the table in front of her and looks at Maria. "It's what you've been seeing."

"It was within a couple of weeks of the gift that I first saw it," Maria says shyly, as if it's hard for her to talk publicly about anything so personal as her visions. "At first I wasn't even sure what it was. I was sitting in this room, and yet suddenly it was as if I was in a far bigger room, as big as the temple, filled with thousands and thousands of people. There were high arches and colored lights. And as I watched, a procession appeared, and—this is what took my breath away—someone held a glittering, jeweled thing, held it high, and it caught the light of the candles. It was very beautiful, and as I watched it, I realized it was a cross. Imagine a cross held aloft in gold and jewels . . . an object of veneration, celebration! And people were singing, and I couldn't understand them, but I knew somehow they were singing about Jesus. And then the picture faded.

"I tried to think what this vision could mean, and I told Martha about it. She said I should wait, and perhaps it would become clear. And one evening, I was sitting here again, and then it was as if I was in the midst of another gathering. We were all outside in the blazing sun, and there were hundreds, no, thousands of people. . . . I could not see the edge of the crowd. Their faces were black, and they stood singing, praising Jesus." Maria smiles as if she has been pulled back into the scene. "My heart has been full from these visions.

"But now I see: perhaps they are for you, Joanna and Mary. For you, as you go to Antioch, and even beyond . . ."

Martha pours a cup of wine in front of her. "New wineskins, new covenant, a whole new way of life that has gathered us to this table. Jesus is with us. That is his promise: he will never fail you nor forsake you."

The women stop, and each sees his blood in her mind's eye, on his arms, feet, the wood, the earth. They remember, and at the same time, they know themselves to be part of the new wine that cannot fit into the old wineskins.

Before they begin to pass the cup, Maria looks around their faces. "But . . ." she begins. Her face changes from the mixture of joy and pain she knows from Jesus to a deep sorrow, and she shakes her head. "Some of the pictures are awful. And then I cannot help but cry. . . . That can't happen, it can't . . . the women . . . Jesus wouldn't let it happen."

They stare as Maria begins to cry inconsolably. "Lost . . . the women, lost, lost," she weeps. They watch her, wondering.

Lost and Found

The women at that table wonder, but we don't. The new wine these women share here in Jerusalem will last for thirty, perhaps forty more years. And then for almost two thousand years, women will be barred from the table, as the church tries desperately to put new wine back into old cracked skins. Maria's prophetic words, Mary Magdalene's apostleship, Joanna's teaching, Martha's celebration of the eucharist, Suheir's evangelism—their leadership in the ministry of the church—swept away, lost. For this we should all weep.

But Maria's weeping fades as if I've turned down a stereo. Martha freezes even as she holds the wine aloft to pour it. "Stop," I say. "Let's have silence in memory of her." In memory of all the women who could not preside at the table—who for many years couldn't even come to the table if they showed signs of their womanhood by being pregnant or menstruating. Let's remember those who have been (and still are) silenced, mourning as we look at the empty chairs—places set by Jesus, but kept empty by the church. We need to mourn these mothers in the faith who should have been our mentors, but were instead bound and gagged.

Women, where are you? According to the Gospels, you stayed faithfully at the cross and went courageously to the tomb that first Easter morning. After all you'd been through with Jesus, your struggle and your commitment, I cannot believe that he somehow slipped your mind—that you decided maybe you'd left the iron on and had better go home and check it. Unlike your male counterparts, you had no alternatives. What town would welcome back a woman who had traveled in mixed company with a suspect rabbi, who had anticipated Martin Luther's suggestion to "let goods and kindred go"? Jesus had turned your lives upside down. The male disciples could go back to their old lives: they had left their nets, but you had burned your boats.

Silenced, forgotten, warped in art: how do we even begin to look for you, our mothers in the faith? This search for clues about missing persons, this scavenger hunt to bring to light "what might well have happened" is a tricky one.

In keeping with the idea of midrash, we turn to the New Testament and begin our search there, reading deeply and comprehensively to see where we can find our foremothers in faith. As we look, we will find more there than meets the eye.

Acts

Where are the women in the book of Acts? They are hidden. When Luke wrote his book, he needed focus to deal with masses of material about a diverse and various movement. Luke chose to write a particular kind of hero story, looking at the new movement as the story of Peter and Paul and the spread of the church through their work. Luke sets the stage for Paul and his missionary journeys by focusing first on the Twelve, then on Peter, and then on Paul—so that the book is named "the Acts of the Apostles," but could be more aptly named "the acts of one apostle" (or two at most). The women (not being Peter and Paul) aren't featured much; even Mary, mother of Jesus, is only mentioned once, before Pentecost. But neither do we see much of several other characters (such as Matthew) who, from their presence in the Gospels, we would expect to see actively involved in the early church.

Epistles

Where are the women in the epistles? Sometimes we forget that the epistles are letters, and that in them Paul was working out various Christian doctrines in specific situations. The fixation on the epistles in many conservative circles (leading to neglect of the Gospels) has led the church to focus on certain culturally specific passages about women speaking, rather than noting the obvious—that women were clearly teaching, prophesying, and praying publicly in the church. Women are referred to in asides and greetings, probably because they weren't creating problems, but instead were actively involved in leadership roles—as apostles, preachers, teachers, and house group leaders.

Gospels

If we think that the women disappeared after the Gospel accounts, we're forgetting that the Gospels were penned after the epistles, so that those Gospel accounts in which women play such a large part were written to people who assumed the active role of women in the church. They are the last word (written in 65–80 c.e.) about women in the early church, reflecting the faith and practice of the Christian community a generation after the crucifixion. The fact that certain women are actively involved in the Gospels means they were well-known ministers in the communities when the Gospels were written.

※

The evidence in the scriptures is hidden, tucked away. But when we look at the scriptures in the light of first-century understandings of women, we see the radical nature of the new movement. If we move from looking at how women were regarded and treated in both Jewish and Greco-Roman society, into the light of the attitudes and actions of Jesus and the Spirit-led earliest church, we find ourselves almost blinded by the contrast.

Largely, then, the task of rescuing the women who have been lost, reconstructing them from these traces, is left to the sanctified and historic imagination.

Women, we need to see and hear you, to know that you didn't give all you had and find yourselves empty-handed. We are ready to listen as we sit with you at this table. Death, time, place—all are meaningless. Knit together, we are in table fellowship. We, too, are women who are struggling to be whole and strong and true to ourselves as we follow the radical, liberating Jesus. Speak to us.

Two

Mary Magdalene

❧

T HE LIGHT FALLS FIRST ON MARY MAGDALENE'S FACE, which seems almost translucent. "From that first morning when I met him alive, I live to tell about him," she says.

I believe Mary Magdalene was an intelligent and sensitive woman in a time when only men could be educated and find challenging vocations. For Mary Magdalene, finding herself fully known and loved by Jesus brought extraordinary freedom and purpose, as the qualities that had made her vulnerable now showed her perceptive and wise. Mary Magdalene stands as an everywoman to contemporary women, calling us into the liberation she experienced in her radical savior. I want to know and be like this woman who gave her life to telling about the light of Jesus (see notes, 95).

We read in the Gospels that Mary Magdalene followed Jesus all over Galilee after he delivered and called her. She stayed by the cross until the end, watching with him as he died. She went to see where the body was laid, and she watched that dark Sabbath with the other women.

And then the tomb on that first Easter: she loved her teacher so deeply that she was willing to risk her life, going to the tomb to care for the body. Mary Magdalene was known in the early church as one of the myrraphores—the ointment bearers who brought spices to anoint the body of Christ. Mary Magdalene met the risen Jesus before anyone else, before any of the male followers, even before he had ascended to God. What electrifying glory, to meet the son of God, newly risen, so freshly hatched that even his father hadn't clapped eyes on him yet! Like his mother's glimpses after his first birthing, Mary Magdalene meets him soaked in glory.

At the tomb, the risen Jesus speaks to her: "Go and tell. . . ." That is how she came to be called "apostle to the apostles," a phrase coined by Hippolytus (170–235 c.e.). Mary Magdalene was a central witness to the resurrection in a time when women's testimony was ill-regarded in a court of law. In earliest Christian art, Mary's discovery in the garden is a favorite theme; when few Christians could read, these murals profoundly taught about the resurrection's first witnesses.

Look at her: Mary Magdalene follows Jesus above all else. She gives herself to the joy and the pain of following him. Jesus says that his true disciples are those whom he calls by name. In the garden, Jesus does just that: "Mary."

Lost

It is just as well, I think, as I look at Mary Magdalene sitting at this table, that she cannot know how she will be lost. What would she think if she knew how her life would be distorted and twisted, made into a caricature?

Mary Magdalene brought news of the risen Lord, but the Twelve considered it to be idle chatter. Who could blame them? They were products of their time. And although the resurrection accounts in the Gospels list Mary Magdalene as the first witness, the "official" account of the resurrection that Paul "received" from the Jerusalem church (1 Corinthians 15:3-8)—a sort of catechism during those first few years—doesn't mention Mary Magdalene. The conservative Jerusalem church, still trying to operate within Judaism's wineskins, would not have mentioned someone who was an invalid witness.

I can understand that an official story in the earliest church might be cautious about who is included as a key witness. But I cannot fathom all else that has happened to Mary Magdalene: when someone refers to this gutsy founder of our faith, we struggle to shut out warped images of her. How could someone as venerable as Mary Magdalene—a model of courage and apostleship in the early church—have been presented to us as a fallen woman, venerated only for her endless sorrow over past sexual sins?

The answer is fairly simple. A church distancing itself from the egalitarian model practiced by Jesus and the primitive church found Mary Magdalene's centrality a major problem. The great church father Origen complained that Mary Magdalene was a "wholly unsuitable first witness." Some church fathers argued that it must have been the mother of Jesus who first met the risen Christ, because it would be clearly inappropriate for Jesus to appear to Mary Magdalene before he appeared to his own mother. Others argued that it was because of their lack of faith that women were the first witnesses. Origen argued that Jesus didn't need to appear to the Blessed Virgin, because she already believed, whereas Mary Magdalene had doubts about his resurrection. In fact, Origen suggested that perhaps Jesus appeared first to Mary Magdalene because the Blessed Virgin asked him to, since the Magdalene had so little faith that she had actually gone to the tomb to anoint a dead body! (Even today, in one of the most popular New Testament translations—the New International Version—a "scholar" suggests in the notes to the resurrection appearance that Jesus probably appeared first to Mary Magdalene because she was upset.) Could it not have been because she was faithful and was there with Jesus—in his ministry, at the cross, and now at the tomb again to anoint him?

The early church, saturated by a patriarchal world, soon found more efficient ways to dispense with Mary Magdalene than questioning her position as first witness to the resurrection. She was fashioned into a fallen woman, confused with the sinful woman who anoints Jesus, and with Mary, sister of Martha (see notes, 95). By the time of Gregory (540–604 C.E.), the damage had been done: these "Marys" were conflated into one person and remained so in official church teaching until 1969. The feast day of the three-in-one is July 22.

Over the years, this catchall Mary Magdalene came to symbolize crucial ideas of asceticism and penitence for the church. Another story was added to these Mary stories—that of Mary of Egypt, a fifth-century harlot who lived a life of sin for seventeen years in Alexandria before working her way to Palestine. There in the desert, she spent forty-seven years repenting for her sins, naked and clothed only in her hair. The similarity of their names and their presumed sins led hagiographers to assume that Mary Magdalene must have done the same to try to get rid of her sinful past—years of naked hirsute penitence. This made-over Mary Magdalene came to symbolize several ideas for the church: no one is beyond grace, but penitence is the key. No longer a strong, forgiven follower of Jesus, an apostle to the apostles, Mary Magdalene's sexual misdeeds led her to a life of penitence, until she was venerated for having eaten and drunk nothing for thirty-two years.

In the transformation of Mary Magdalene to a penitent *par excellence,* we see more about the attitudes of an ascetic church than we do about the woman herself: at the heart of the church's asceticism was a horror about sex and the body. Eve was blamed for the fall, from the period after about 200 c.e., and it seemed clear to early theologians that Eve ate, not of the tree of the knowledge of good and evil as the scripture says, but of the tree of carnal knowledge. Replacing the teachings of Paul (that celibacy might be an option for some), sex, except for the begetting of a child, was seen as bad. Sexual sin came to be linked with the fall: sex led to expulsion from the garden and to death, with woman as the responsible party. Without death, sex wouldn't be necessary, and thus sex, death, and the female were intertwined. Mary Magdalene's name became synonymous with the dangers and degradations of the flesh. Years after she had met the risen Christ, she still wandered in the desert trying to make up for her sexual sins.

As Mary Magdalene became a favorite model of asceticism and penitence, many bodies worth of her relics turned up, and stories of her life and death became popular reading, the sexy novels of their time. Virginity was the ideal—in a book of saints, women are referred to by whether or not they are virgins—and Mary Magdalene provided a steamy alternative, and one who even through years of penitence could never quite recover from her past life.

Mary Magdalene ceased to be one of us and became ever penitent, never able to atone for her moral lapses before she met Jesus; she is portrayed in art looking endlessly depressed about her body and the way it has led her astray. Most of us are not living lives of complete sexual depravity, and even if we were, Mary Magdalene's cure doesn't appeal—years and years of complete fasting, naked in the desert, to try to make oneself good enough for God. Warped in art, ignored in sermons and Bible studies, lost to us as a mentor and ideal: the Mary Magdalene of the church's making bears no relationship to the Mary Magdalene of the Gospel accounts.

How do we find her when she seems to be missing in action? Look, the writer of Isaiah says, to the rock from which you were hewn, the quarry from which you were dug.

Found

We look to you, Mary Magdalene, as one who followed Jesus, a disciple in darkness as well as in light. We listen to you—apostle to the apostles—who carried the message of Jesus.

Mary Magdalene may disappear in the book of Acts, but her significant role in the Gospels speaks of her importance in the early church. In those early days before the written word, witnesses to the life and resurrection of Jesus were valued for their teaching, and Mary Magdalene was the key witness to the resurrection.

From what I see of Mary Magdalene in the Gospel accounts, I believe that she would have stayed in Jerusalem after Pentecost, preaching and teaching. After the stoning of Stephen, I suspect that she and Joanna went off to Antioch, where they might have felt at home with the more Spirit-led Hellenistic Christian believers in the rich, diverse community there. Ultimately, I expect she traveled further, spreading the message to Rome. Stories tell of her getting to France, but it doesn't really matter whether those are fact or myth: she carried on her apostolic work until she died.

The light catches Mary Magdalene's eyes, and she looks around the table. "Tell us, Mary. What was it like when you found him alive?" Susannah squeezes Mary Magdalene's hand. Most of these women have heard the story many times, but they will never tire of it. Suheir has never heard it. And we, as contemporary women, want to hear the story in her own words.

"I would love to," Mary says. She pauses for a minute or two and allows the familiar room and faces to take her back to that most momentous morning. For Mary, and for all after who follow the rabbi, that morning changed the world from darkness to light. Christian worship is held on Sunday—the first day of the week—because of Mary Magdalene's discovery that morning.

❧

WE WORRIED SO MUCH about him those last few months, and that last week, I had watched him move toward death. Then he was arrested and killed. You can't imagine . . . Suheir, all that night we told our stories, how we'd met him and he'd changed us . . . trying desperately, we were, to understand how someone like Jesus could be dead. We talked and cried and sat in silence.

When first light touched the sky's edges, we set off through the chill air, holding spices to anoint his body.

Lifetimes had passed since we had left the town on Friday— could it have been only thirty-six hours before?—since we'd laid his body to rest.

But it was only as we entered the garden that Joanna remembered the tomb was sealed, and we wouldn't be able to open it. Maybe she could ask the soldiers, Mary Clopas suggested, but Joanna said it would be too dangerous to ask about a criminal. . . .

How could she care, I wondered. With Jesus dead, it didn't matter what else happened. . . . If we were seized and killed . . .

No fear, no hope . . . there was nothing, but even that didn't seem to matter. All that mattered was each step, bringing me closer to his dear body, all that was left of the one I loved. Walking through that gray dawn, each step towards him . . . that was all there was.

A bird chirped in the distance. I heard my own breathing, our footsteps. Closer . . . closer . . .

And then we were there, and it was all wrong . . . the stone yanked out of the way. Joanna pulled me back. "Wait here," she said, and pushed in to look. She turned, her face twisted. "Gone," she whispered. "Gone."

I ran, sobbing wildly. How . . . how could this happen? My beloved teacher, my friend . . . dead. Was it too much to ask that I be able to touch his body, anoint him, and tell him I loved him? Each step had been toward him . . . I needed him.

The horror of those next minutes, or hours . . . I felt myself falling as the last thread holding me in my new life tore . . . not even the body. My hands longed more than anything to touch his cold flesh. . . .

I lay curled on the grass, sobbing. . . . If I could see him . . . one last time. I tried to remind myself: he never meant to leave you alone, no, he was just too good. . . . We'd known they would kill him, but he didn't understand.

You still have your love for him, I told myself . . . love is as strong as death . . . but I wanted to touch him. I sobbed and sobbed, and my world was black.

Vandals, grave robbers, those cruel jokers who had laughed by the cross . . . "If you're the son of God, climb down from there. . . . Hey, miracle worker, not feeling so great?" What were they doing to him now?

O God . . . and then it seemed to me that I understood. God was like them—the grave robbers, vandals, cruel jokers. . . .

The sickest joke of all was this God. Jesus loved "his father"—that's what he called him, and look how God cared for him. . . . This God abandoned Jesus in his greatest need. . . . His cry echoed in my head: "My God, my God, why have you forsaken me?" I pulled my veil over my head to hide from the horror. The nightmare of a sun rising on a world where there was no Jesus and no loving God, no hope.

How much time passed, I don't know. Finally, I pulled myself to my feet. Where were the others? How could I go back and tell his mother that his body had been stolen?

I turned toward the tomb. . . . Where were the spices? I'd dropped them somewhere. "Where is he, where is he?" I stumbled. It seemed that if I found the spices, maybe I'd find the body. "Please, please," I wept.

Like a person in a nightmare, I was wiping my face and eyes with my veil and trying to see the jar. . . .

And then there was someone there.

Maybe he'll know, I thought. He asked why I was crying. "Have you seen him?" I sobbed. "I've got to find him . . . please . . . help me."

"Mary." That split second, it seemed to me that the trees froze, dropped their leaves, and burst into blossom. The old sun died in the sky, and a new, young sun leapt up. The constellations wheeled, the Southern Cross shoving the Big Dipper out of the way. "Mary." Jesus had always called me that.

Time stopped. He was dead, I knew that. . . . I had watched the whole process from beginning to end, seen them take his dead body from the cross; I had touched his cold flesh, helped to lay him in the tomb. Oh yes, he was dead, and yet . . . I wiped away my tears beyond tears. There . . . his dearly remembered jawbone running from ear to ear, and the lines at the sides of his eyes. His voice. "Mary."

My old name for him choked into my mouth: "Rabboni." I wanted to hug him and bury my head on his chest, trace the lines of his precious feet. His eyes crinkled, and he laughed as my tears overflowed again, but now from joy. "Mary," he said. "Mary."

I walked back to Bethany, crying and laughing and skipping. I stepped in the door, and sad, brave faces turned to me. Martha spoke, "Joanna said there was a problem . . . that we forgot about the stone."

Susannah, it was you who really looked at me. "Mary! What is it? What's happened?"

"I've seen him. Jesus. I've seen him. He said, 'Mary.'"

I looked at you, Martha, and you, Maria. "Do you hear what I'm saying? He's not dead."

Maria, you hugged me. "Are you sure? You're tired; it's been a rough few days."

Martha, you were shaking your head: "She's so high-strung. . . ."

I ran over to where his mother was sitting and hugged her. "He's alive. Death couldn't hold him. My sisters, he's alive, and I've spoken to him." I looked into all your faces. "I thought he was the gardener! And then he said, "Mary," just like he always did. The first word he ever spoke to me . . . Mary.

"But I'm forgetting!" I said. "He told me I needed to tell the others. I had to tell you first, but now I need to tell the men. . . . I wonder if they'll believe me." I ran to the place they were staying as I'd never run before. I felt as if I'd heard the songs of heaven with the ears of earth: I had been cracked open by glory.

They looked terrible, and when I told them, they tried to be polite. Peter didn't even look up, just sat with his head in his hands. I'm sure they felt bad about not having been there at the execution, and I said I thought Jesus would come to them soon, and then one of them said that if something extraordinary like this were going to happen, Jesus would have the sense to use someone who could at least be a witness in a court of law. I almost laughed out loud; I felt as if nothing could ever make me sad again—every time I closed my eyes even halfway, I could see the face of Jesus.

I came back to this room and curled up and slept all that day and through the night. At about nine in the evening, John knocked to tell us that Jesus had come to them, and he especially wanted to tell me. I smiled at him, and then I slept again.

During the next weeks, we slept, cooked, talked, and remembered. Jesus told us that he would be leaving, that he would give us a gift better than his physical presence, the very breath of who he was.

That's the story, and I've been telling it ever since, to anyone who will listen. It is my life: to walk wherever Jesus calls me and tell others that death and darkness are not as powerful as life and light.

Three

Maria, Sister of Martha

❧

MARIA LOOKS UP FROM HER PLACE by Martha and speaks to the gathered women. "The Spirit gives us joy and makes us strong to walk with Jesus, to know his heart."

Lost

Known in the Gospels as Mary, sister of Martha, I call her Maria to set her apart from the plethora of Marys who followed Jesus, and it's true that all those Marys have confused people down the centuries (see notes, 96). Most contemporary individuals, even those who have spent plenty of time in pews, know little about this one, except perhaps that she sat at Jesus' feet when Martha didn't. Our response to her may be, "Mary who?" Maria has disappeared, largely forgotten.

I see Maria as a follower of Jesus blessed with a deeper understanding than many other followers—the kind of woman who pays close attention and then figures out where the wisdom is, what the real emotions are. She was always several jumps ahead of the male disciples.

When we see Maria in Luke's Gospel, she seems to be the only one who understands how crucial the words of Jesus are; she joyfully listens to them, sitting at the feet of the rabbi. Jesus commends her, affirming that Maria has made the better choice.

Although Jesus commends Maria, it's easy for us to think that she had it easy. Which one of us wouldn't choose to sit and listen to a great teacher while someone else made dinner? But if we stop to consider this scene more closely, we must acknowledge Maria's courage. Even for women today, Maria's choice would be a hard one, but with societal pressures being what they were, for her to sit and learn could only have been a deliberate and difficult choice that should stand as a challenge to us.

Maria, sitting there at Jesus' feet, must have been very well aware that her sister was unhappy. If I'd been Maria and heard my sister slamming cupboard doors and snorting in the kitchen, I would have said, "Jesus, you know this is absolutely fascinating, but I think I'll have to excuse myself; it sounds like my sister needs me to give her a little hand in the kitchen." Yet Maria doesn't get up.

Even more insistent than her sister's distress, Maria would have heard voices that echoed back to her childhood, criticizing her for sitting at a rabbi's feet. As Maria knew only too well, as a woman, she was considered to be like a child, incapable of moral or ethical decisions. Maria would have known the common teaching at the time: for a woman to be taught the holy scriptures was like giving them pornography; the Torah should rather be burned than given to a woman. Maria would have known that before Jesus, no rabbi had ever called women, taught them, and allowed them to follow him. So here is Maria—doing something remarkable in just sitting at the feet of Jesus. No wonder Jesus salutes her for her choice. To me and other contemporary women, Maria stands as one who knows what she values and holds faithfully to it in defiance of societal pressures (see notes, 96).

Maria likely remained at the cross when the others had scattered. We imagine the crucifixion as we've seen it in paintings—men, women, and patrons of the arts standing around watching. But according to the Gospels, it is the women who were there (see notes, 97).

And for them, it was not only horrific to see him tortured (and to witness his nakedness, which in that culture was shame indeed), it was also dangerous to be seen mourning at the cross of a criminal. Their memories of that Good Friday are memories of an endless nightmare.

Before that dreadful day, near the end of John's Gospel, it is Maria who is most keenly aware that Jesus will die. Sensing his fear and loneliness, she shows her love by anointing her teacher. Jesus commends her again: this moment is so profound that Jesus says her anointing will be told as a part of his story, told in memory of her. In the early church, Maria, Mary Magdalene, Joanna, and Salome were all myrraphores who carried ointment to anoint Jesus. Maria stands for courage, sensitivity, and loving action. The writer of the book of John refers to Maria as one whom Jesus loved.

Maria stands as one of the great disciples, one who understood, followed, and loved. Why, then, has she not been held up for our emulation throughout the history of the church?

Maria was somehow misplaced, confused with other characters by the church fathers. Linked with Mary Magdalene and the sinful woman who anointed Jesus, Maria was conflated into a symbol, not of a woman's strength, understanding, and courage, but of women's fleshly weakness, shame, and unending penitence. Contemporary Catholic scholars believe that there must have been a willful misunderstanding to confuse the three on the part of earlier teachers, and it's hard to see how it could have been other than intentional. The "sinful woman"—the prostitute who anoints Jesus—was not driven to prostitution by rebelliousness or carnality (as were her customers) but by desperate poverty. This woman could not have been the same as the woman who owned, with her sister, a house in Bethany. If this mistake was not intentional, it was highly motivated by a subconscious need to disgrace the women followers of Jesus.

And so another powerful model and mentor, one who stands for courageous defiance of societal pressures, one who listens to Jesus, and one who is repeatedly commended by her teacher, is sexualized and given the Sisyphean task of endlessly repenting for sexual sins. Jesus says the story of her anointing will be told in memory of her, but we've proved Jesus wrong, as all memory of Maria has been effectively wiped out for nearly two thousand years.

Found

Maria, we remember you. We welcome your early vision of truth gleaned from hours of sitting at the feet of Jesus, your clear expression of love for the teacher, and your steadfastness as you held close to him to the end. We as women claim you as a mother of the church (see notes, 97).

Sensitive, wise, Spirit filled—speak to us, Maria.

Jesus told us to wait. After he was gone, we were drawn to that room in the city. We prayed, talked, and read the scriptures.

Watching and waiting: women are good at these things, I guess. Certainly Martha and I learned it the hard way after Lazarus died. Perhaps it was easier for us. We had no idea what we were waiting for, but I tried to remind myself that if it was from Jesus, it would be good.

I watched the men and wondered what would happen to them. I remembered those first days after Jesus was raised when they seemed paralyzed by guilt, not only at having abandoned Jesus, but in not believing, not understanding. When Jesus first came to them, they were so scared they had locked the doors, and John told me that Jesus called them foolish and slow of heart.

I think Peter felt he didn't deserve the joy of Jesus alive, and I watched him as he prayed in that room, poring over the scriptures. One day he got the idea that somebody ought to replace Judas. He made an announcement about the criteria—someone who had walked with them and met the risen Jesus.

Joanna and I looked at each other. Clearly it didn't cross Peter's mind that the most likely candidate was the first witness herself, who had been given the message to take to the men that first morning. Peter felt very responsible and terrified of making another mistake, and he seemed to forget that Jesus had chosen some pretty unlikely people, himself included. Peter drew lots, and Matthias was elected. I'm not sure what happened to him. I had to remind myself that they were trying to be conscientious and faithful, but they hadn't really glimpsed the radical nature of the new movement.

How could they? We knew the extraordinary cost to Jesus. Others might discuss how much Jesus understood about his death and resurrection, but I remembered the anguish in his eyes that night at our house when I anointed him. He knew he would die, but he didn't know how he would handle the pain; he didn't know for sure what would happen afterwards.

Peter and the others hadn't been there at the cross. Seared into my mind forever was this brutal image of Jesus naked, shamed, and in agony on the cross. Our loving Lord . . . we, the women who watched him, we knew that Jesus had reversed everything, turned all upside down. As outcasts, as the weak, we understood what it was to worship a God who had chosen weakness and flesh.

And so we waited and prayed. Jerusalem was full of people gathered for the feast of Pentecost. Then it finally happened.

We were there as usual that morning. Some of the believers were eating, talking quietly, or praying. I had just settled down to pray, and I heard donkey hooves from the street outside, the voice of someone intoning a psalm.

Suddenly there was a terrible noise, a roaring, and it flashed through my mind that it was an earthquake, torrential rain, or thunder. People leapt to their feet, screamed, cried out. . . .

A split second after we heard the sound, we were hit by a mighty wind. I felt the wind slam my back and then tear around my whole body, lofting my arms and legs. I opened my mouth and gulped the wind that hit my face, pushing back my eyelashes. It was like being at the seashore when a wave catches your feet, tumbling and washing you.

As I swung around, I thought of a great dance with no pattern, but tremendous beauty. I caught sight of Thomas, who was staring upwards, hands up, swaying, at Jesus' mother, who had her veil pushed back and was swinging around slowly. And as the dance went on, there seemed to be sparks carried by the wind, flitting above people's heads, glittering and moving.

This was the promise: none of us doubted. This was God—the Great Spirit enveloping and overwhelming us. We were swept along in a torrent of the deepest joy imaginable, palpable within and without; we were dancing in joy, leaping in a blustering sense of being loved. I was strong; I could have run up a mountain.

And then I saw that the others were laughing and crying, some hugging each other, and I realized I was laughing and crying. And when I tried to speak to Mark, who was near me, he was laughing, and I could not understand what he was saying, but it didn't seem to matter. We were floating in God, drenched in God: no one was going to ask questions. All we could do was dance this wild dance and laugh and cry.

I swung around, dizzy from swimming in God, and it was as if there was glitter everywhere, like raindrops when the sun has come out, glistening and flashing.

And then it seemed that the room could no longer hold us, and we started tumbling down the stairs, clapping each other on the back, clutching hands. When we got onto the street, a crowd stared at us. Some began dragging family members away. "Drunk," they said.

Then—and this would have seemed very odd, but it didn't somehow, because of all that had happened in the last fifteen minutes (or was it fifteen hours?)—Peter stood on the top step, and he started to speak, laughing and telling them that it was too early to be drunk. And then Peter gave a most wonderful sermon.

He spoke about the prophet Joel, and the Spirit poured out on us, and about how this was God's plan. The Spirit was not just for the prophets, but for everyone, for all flesh. And then he mentioned Jesus, and it was as if he saw it all. Jesus' teaching, his power to heal and forgive as a seamless garment with his death, his resurrection, and now this gift that they were seeing and hearing. The Spirit was proof of Jesus' truth, Peter said.

People began to weep and pull veils over their faces; some ripped their clothing and began to wail, "What can we do?" Hundreds (though some said thousands) joined the fellowship. You can imagine the chaos, and all of us who knew the words of Jesus were needed to teach the new believers.

Life since that day has been life in the Spirit, Jesus here with us, as he was when he sat in the living room here at Bethany. It wasn't long after that day that I started seeing the visions.

Four

Mary, Mother of Jesus

❧

T HE LIGHT SHIFTS TO A FACE WE'VE SEEN in stained glass, fine art, and kitsch—Mary, mother of Jesus. "We are given the extraordinary privilege of collaborating with God," she says, looking around the women gathered at this table.

As the light falls on her face, I wonder. This woman, a struggling follower who waited with the other disciples for the Spirit at Pentecost, what outrage would she feel if she could see how she would be changed in art and doctrine, her garbled image used to oppress women? She would prefer, I suspect, her treatment by the Protestant branch of the church, where she's been buried and forgotten.

I believe Mary, mother of Jesus, has much to teach us about collaboration—about saying yes to God. But we must dig through thick layers of myth to even begin to find her.

Lost

There are few scriptural references to Mary (see notes, 97). In fact, the key doctrines of the Catholic church about Mary are unrelated to (and arguably contrary) to the witness of scripture. Of the four dogmas that the church has declared—the virgin birth, the assumption, the immaculate conception, her divine motherhood—only one is even vaguely alluded to in Scripture. These doctrines tell us little about Mary, but a lot about the desires of the church.

While affirming Mary's virginity when she bore Jesus, I would argue with the way the church has extended it and emphasized it; in her treatment by the church, Mary became more of a symbol of virginity than a living, breathing woman who said yes to God. The virginity of Mary became a key issue to the church fathers, despite the fact that scholars aren't sure whether the Old Testament passage— "behold a virgin shall conceive and bear a son" (Isaiah 7:14)—refers to someone who has never had intercourse or simply to a young woman. The exaltation of virginity is completely foreign to the Jewish culture in which Mary (and Jesus) lived; in that milieu, barrenness, widowhood, or lack of marriage are indications of a curse, not something to be lauded (see notes, 98-99).

Luke and Matthew are closer to that Jewish understanding. Neither writer emphasizes Mary's virginity; they imply that she consummated her marriage with Joseph, and they refer to other children. And yet the church came to hold the doctrine that Mary was *virgo intacta post partum*—not only spared sex, but also allowed by God to never lose her virginity, even in bearing Jesus. (For some time, the church fathers speculated that the brothers referred to in Scripture must have been Joseph's children by a former marriage; by the time of Jerome, Joseph was declared to be a virgin also, and therefore a truly holy man.)

Although the idea of virgin birth was not unknown in Roman understanding (generally as an indication of deity), the myths surrounding the virgin Mary were unique in the way they were used as propaganda to support the church's growing asceticism. The church's agenda was coupled with apocryphal texts (most influentially *The Book of James*) to fashion a straw woman.

In *The Book of James*, Joachim is a very good and charitable man, married to the virtuous Anna; they are unable to have children, so Joachim goes into the desert to pray while Anna remains at home. An angel appears to both of them, telling them that their prayers have been answered, and Mary is born.

Anna dedicates Mary to the temple, and her childhood is attended by miracles, such as her walking seven steps at six months. Mary is taken to the temple at age three, where she serves for ten years in the sanctuary. (No female would ever have been allowed this close to the Holy of Holies, of course.) The high priest then becomes concerned about the sanctuary of the Lord being polluted by Mary (presumably because she might begin menstruating at any time), and so he calls all the widowers in the area to vie for her hand. They each carry a rod, and Joseph's bursts into blossom, showing that he is to be her husband. As an old man, he is willing to leave her intact.

Mary weaves a sacred veil for the temple, a task she can do since she is undefiled before God. When she finds she is pregnant, she and Joseph go through a test (prescribed in the book of Numbers) of drinking bitter waters, and they are shown to be chaste.

At the actual birth, Mary kneels and brings forth Jesus. A woman named Salome, skeptical that Mary could still be a virgin after childbirth, examines her. She yelps as her hand is burnt for her lack of faith. She pleads for forgiveness and is healed by holding the baby Jesus.

Ideas about Mary's virginity and the annunciation are not only surrounded by myth, but are further complicated by shifting understandings of the gender of the Holy Spirit, as well as developing ideas about human generation. The Spirit, scholars argue, shifted from feminine to masculine: the Spirit of God, *Shekinah*, was feminine in Hebrew; neuter in Greek *(pneuma)*; feminine as the Greek *sophia*, wisdom; feminine in Syriac; and in Latin, which was becoming the *lingua franca*, it was masculine *(spiritus sanctus)*. Societal understanding of the gender of the Spirit affected a society's understanding of what happened at the annunciation.

Add to this mix shifting ideas of human generation. Tertullian (influenced by the Stoics) believed that the whole person was present in semen; this idea is evident in art showing Mary as a "bake oven" for the loaf, put in her by the (male) Spirit.

Aristotle saw woman as providing the lowly matter (in her menstrual blood) that was given a higher life (spirit and motion) by the man's seed. Aquinas followed Aristotelian biology, considering woman to be incubator or blood transfuser of the divine life. In this understanding of human generation, the annunciation becomes like the creation in Genesis, where the Spirit of God breathes life into dust, making a living soul. Woman, in this view, is despised for her association with matter, flesh, and the carnal.

In Greek understanding, women were fleshly and low; the prime role of women in the Jewish religion was to help men fulfill their covenantal obligations, but they were largely regarded as dangerous sources of pollution. They were exempt from daily prayer and religious rituals, but they held very strictly to laws of ritual purity, including menstrual purity, violations of which were thought to lead to death in childbirth.

These attitudes toward women seeped into the fledgling Christian faith, moving the church to exalt virginity. Women, associated with the flesh, caused the fall, acted as accomplices of Satan, and led to the downfall of men. Eve was cursed to bear children, and her flesh drags men down into the mud. According to the church fathers, this was woman. Augustine wrote of the feces and urine of childbirth, and of menstruation, which made women animal-like. "The whole of her bodily beauty," St. John Chrysostom warned, "is nothing less than phlegm, blood, bile, rheum, and the fluid of digested food." Distaste for women's flesh and blood was not atypical at the time, but using it as propaganda was: we see this clearly in the marketing of Mary, as the church moved from "virgin birth to virginity, from religious sign to moral doctrine," Warner suggests, making Mary into an instrument of asceticism and female subjection. From Augustine, these three are inextricably bound—the sinfulness of sex, the virgin birth, and the great good of virginity.

Women were associated with flesh, and therefore with sex, and thus with sin. Satan came to be portrayed as female (see, for instance, the Sistine Chapel) and the fall was into sexual sin. Without the fall, there would be no death and no sex. St. John Chrysostom argued that the fall was the cause of marriage: "For where there is death, there too is sexual coupling; and where there is no death, there is no sexual coupling either." Other theologians disagreed, like

Augustine and Aquinas, at least on whether Adam and Eve had sex, arguing that if they had not had intercourse, God would not have needed to create woman, because obviously a man would be better as a companion. Prelapsarian intercourse, however, would have been unstained by passion. With the fall, Augustine argues, Adam and Eve covered their genitals, because they understood that the fall had brought the great evil of passion into the world.

During the church's discussions on the nature of Christ in the fourth and fifth centuries, ideas about Mary's virginity were key, but it was at the Fourth Lateran Council that Pope Martin declared Mary's perpetual virginity to be a doctrine of the church. This doctrine was necessary: if woman is evil, the woman who bore Jesus must have been entirely different. Mary, ever virgin, becomes the second Eve, the one who reverses the fall's results.

Mary was gradually becoming less and less human—she doesn't sin, doesn't have sex, doesn't have labor pains, and after a few years, she wasn't allowed to lactate. And yet she is one who feels: she cries. (During the time of the Black Death, Jesus was seen as a judge, but Mary, who knew what it was to lose a son, was the one you could go to with your sorrow.)

Soon it was not enough that Mary was ever virgin; she had to have been untainted by original sin itself. In the doctrine of original sin (that all are tainted by and predisposed to sin), the curse was believed to be transmitted to babies because of their mothers' past sexual acts. Although it was only in 1854 that the immaculate conception became an official doctrine of the church, it had been developing for some time. Mary was made into a person conceived without sin and therefore the only human creature not subject to original sin. God had chosen her as a beloved daughter from the beginning of time, placing her in her mother Anna's womb.

Although the scriptures tell us nothing about the death of Mary, sex and death became so closely related in the understanding of Mary (and of virtue) that people began to argue that she could not have died a normal death. Following the doctrine of the immaculate conception, Mary's bodily assumption was made a doctrine of the church in 1954. Since Mary did not allow her body to be corrupted by sex, she is given the ultimate reward for holiness—no death.

At her assumption, Mary becomes queen of heaven, an image that has become intertwined with apocryphal figures from the book of Revelation—for example, the New Jerusalem adorned as a bride, the church. As queen of heaven, Mary became one with these goddesslike beings, and yet, somehow, also the bride of Christ and the beloved of monks and priests entering the church.

Medieval troubadours sang songs of holy passion within the rules of courtly love, pledging themselves to a lady unavailable to them. This courtly love could never be consummated; chastity was part of the burning fire that made the love holy. This troubadour love was taken and made over into love for the virgin queen of heaven, and she became known as Notre Dame (our lady). The knight was encouraged to give all his chaste but burning love to Mary.

Mary also came to embody the virtues of humility and compliance: "Let it be to me according to your word" (Luke 1:38), she says to the angel, and although humility and gentleness are Christian virtues embodied in both Jesus and Mary, they are largely seen as feminine ones. Especially in largely Catholic countries, machismo is the province of men, while women submit, withdraw, and are praised for their Mary-like goodness. As humility and docility are associated with the virgin, they are demanded of women. Both the church and the churlish husband have benefited from this docile, self-giving model. Only if you are ever virgin and ever mother (and untainted by original sin, not to mention made of plaster) might you be good enough to win a place near the altar in the Catholic or Orthodox church (see notes, 98-99).

As a strong woman who chose personal and spiritual growth, Mary has been lost to us, elevated onto a distant pedestal in the doctrines of the Catholic church.

But she has also been lost to the Protestant church. Sixteenth-century reformers felt that believers were right in looking up to and honoring Mary, but they spoke out against the invocation of Mary rather than Jesus. They rejected traditions about Mary not substantiated in Scripture, and then went further by reacting to the cult of Mary by ignoring her, removing from us a woman model and mentor.

Whether we are Protestant, Catholic, or not Christian at all, paintings and sculptures of Mary—docile and demure, weeping gently, curtsying before an angel, looking at the body of her dead son—are powerfully printed on our minds.

Can we replace that passive image with another? Imagine Mary as a human being, not ever virgin, but ever seeking God, struggling with the pains and stresses of all human women. It is that Mary who has something to teach us.

Found

Mary, you are not completely other; you are like us. Step off your lonely pedestal. Sit with us, because you are one of us. Jesus himself said you were not to be honored as simply breasts and womb, but as a follower. You, Mary, joined our same struggle: to keep moving and growing throughout life. You were there at the cross and in the upper room after Jesus' death and resurrection, waiting for the promised Holy Spirit. You know what it is to actively collaborate with God.

Why did God choose you? God must have seen a woman who loved fully, who was strong enough for growth, who was open to a life of adventure.

Mary, of the millions of prayers that have floated toward you down the ages, please listen to this one. Speak to us about how you lived your life after your son's death. Myths told tales of you dying daily of grief, daily reliving his crucifixion. But I think that you were there taking the word you'd heard and borne, bearing it once again to a wider world. Mary, speak.

I AM HAPPY to sit at this table. Early, early, God taught me to value the women he had placed in my life. When the angelic presence first came to me, asking me to play my part in bringing Jesus into the world . . . even then, before an answer was required of me, I was told of Elizabeth's pregnancy. God knows, my sisters, better than we ourselves, that we need the encouragement and support of others if we are to follow God's call. We cannot do it by ourselves. What a wonderful gift—sharing with someone who was also great with child, and pregnant as I was with joy and fear. God spoke to me as clearly through Elizabeth as he had through the angel.

After Joseph's death, I allowed myself to lean on my sisters again, especially as we traveled from Galilee and were with Jesus that last week. The horror of his death still haunts me, but I began to realize that with your help, my sisters, I could bear and do almost anything. And so in my life in the new community I have continued to encourage, to teach and minister.

Through you, my sisters, I have known what it is to be loved. Just as Jesus wouldn't allow me to hide, wouldn't let me be simply womb and breasts, you, my sisters, would never love me simply as his mother. The days when I carried or suckled him—I cannot consider those years to be the highest in my life. Challenged by you, I keep growing and learning, loving and following.

Jesus despised the way we put people into little parcels of expectation, the way we allow others' demands of us to become an idolatry. I had to walk away from that. I understand now the wisdom of what he said, that we who follow are indeed family.

Like you, my sisters, I am called, called to speak because of all I've learned. Since the earliest days, I've had a habit of wondering, of taking all that happens and turning it over, like a loaf of bread—kneading it and waiting for it to rise.

There were years when I struggled to do that, the dreadful years when I let fear overtake me, when instead of pondering I fled from my thoughts. My heart grew cold whenever I thought about

*my son, my life, my choices. Fear . . . it stifles growth. All you can do
is build a little wall around your heart. And I did that. All those
fearful years.*

*And yet I kept tucking my thoughts away, hiding them within the
bastion of my heart. Before he died—when I'd come to terms with his
life and calling—during that time, I saw his life afresh. I saw that we
are all called to grow up. Jesus was, I was, we all are. And as we grow
up, we are to find our own ways of belonging, ministering, and following. For me, the gift of the Spirit has sealed that message and put
it deep within my heart.*

*We walk with God and with the Spirit, moment by moment. We
wake in the Spirit, we go to sleep in the Spirit, we speak in the Spirit.
For all of us, it is a life of carrying God. God within us now, closer
than close. That is why we can trust.*

*When I said yes to the angel, yes to God that day, I said yes, but
not to something happening to me. Not to a passive acceptance of
God, but to a dance. I'm not sure I understood that . . . but my life
from that day has been a dance with God.*

*And all our lives are that—a dance with God. You know when the
marriage dance begins and everyone finds their places and begins to
move. That's what God is like. All who can walk are drawn into the
dance. Just as I was with God—God growing, God born, God muddy-
ing my floors, God speaking to me, me speaking to God. God pulling
away, God coming back, God calling me to more than I ever thought I
could do. It is true for me and my life; it is true for all who choose to
dance with God. I teach God, and God teaches me.*

*You have all heard of that day at Cana when I pushed Jesus. It
seemed to me that it was time, time for a new part of the dance. I realized as I sat—swept up in the joy of the wedding feast—that I was con-
tent. I wanted the dance to stay as it was, Jesus working in the
carpenter shop at Nazareth, reading, thinking, growing under my loving eyes. I feasted my eyes on him as he chatted with a couple of friends
across the room. . . . And it was as I watched him that my cousin came
to me, her face drawn, to tell me they were out of wine. And I knew: for
Jesus, for me, a new part of the dance was to begin.*

I went over and spoke to him, and he looked strangely at me, as if he was remembering something long forgotten. "Woman" he called me . . . then he looked excited and a bit frightened, like a woman looks as she goes into labor—afraid of the pain, excited about the baby's birth, overwhelmed by the future. I turned to the servants. "Do whatever he tells you."

I sat down again, and it crashed over me. What had I done? The sword that Simeon had prophesied turned in my heart. There was no turning back; the quiet life of Nazareth was over. The dance had changed, and all was different.

Afterward I wondered why I had pushed him . . . but I came to see that it was necessary, because that's what God is like. We are not made to be passive watchers, but fully, deeply involved in encouraging each other to do the work of God. That moment at Cana took my pushing, Jesus acting, and the servants filling. It was a new dance, wilder than the one we'd known.

At a house meeting a week or two ago, someone told a story about Jesus that I'd never heard. He was near Tyre when a woman started following him around, asking him to cast a demon out of her daughter, and the male disciples got so annoyed that they asked Jesus to send her away. Jesus spoke to the woman, telling her that he couldn't, because he was called to God's chosen people. And she answered, "But even the dogs get to eat the crumbs that fall from the master's table." She pushed him, and he responded, and her daughter was healed. Right there, the dance was expanded. Perhaps it is because of that woman that Jesus was able to stop and include Suheir and her village in the dance.

The song God gave me when I was pregnant means more and more to me, because it is a song of what God is like. From childhood, Hannah's song had troubled and inspired me. How would I respond to such a call from God; what would it be like to give my firstborn to God's service as Hannah had? When I was with Elizabeth that day, the song bubbled out of me. Hannah's song had become my song:

Sing out, my soul,
sing of the holiness of God:
who has delighted in a woman,
lifted up the poor,
satisfied the hungry,
given voice to the silence,
grounded the oppressor,
blessed the full-bellied with emptiness,
and with the gift of tears
those who have never wept;
who has desired the darkness of the womb,
and inhabited our flesh.
Sing of the longing of God,
sing out, my soul.

I love to teach my song to the new community, because it is about who God is and how God works.

Five

Joanna

J OANNA STIRS IN HER PLACE next to Mary Magdalene. "We cling
to nothing in our following. Remember, he said, 'Anyone who
puts hand to plow and looks back does not belong.' Jerusalem,
comfort, life . . . they are nothing as we follow Jesus. In him, all is
made new."

In the New Testament, Joanna is mentioned by name only
twice. Luke describes her as one who supported Jesus out of her
resources and one who went to the tomb. This means she was one of
the anonymous "women from Galilee" mentioned in all of the
Gospel accounts, who followed Jesus during his life and stayed with
him at his death (see notes, 99).

With this lack of biblical material, is it any wonder Joanna is
lost? Yet there are other characters who seldom appear in the scriptures, but are household names, like Zacchaeus or Bartimaeus.

Lost

Joanna is lost, I think, because she is disturbing, a challenge to many
ideas we hold dear. Hers is the kind of challenge I would prefer to
sidestep. In her intelligence and experience, Joanna seems to have
been able to cut to the heart of the faith.

Luke tells us that Joanna was the wife of Herod's steward, Chuza, and that she followed Jesus in Galilee, providing for him. Scholars figure that Joanna would have been the most sophisticated and educated of the women (or perhaps of all Jesus' followers). Living in Herod's household, she would have been fluent in Greek and Aramaic and used to the sophistication of court life—the fancy parties, political intrigues, and celebrities.

The court that Joanna abandoned to follow Jesus was known to be decadent. It is unclear whether Joanna was present when Herodias's daughter danced, and Herod was so "moved" by her dancing that he delivered John the Baptist's head on a platter. But the immorality and debauchery of that household would have been her normal milieu before she met Jesus. Joanna would have been used to the idea of Herod having married his brother's wife, which John preached against, bringing disfavor on himself.

Joanna is never referred to as a widow, there is no record of Chuza having died, and it was extremely unusual for a woman in this culture not to have children. Scholars believe that there's a good chance Joanna left her husband and family to follow Jesus.

In his great hymn, "A Mighty Fortress Is Our God," Martin Luther suggests that Christians "Let goods and kindred go, / This mortal life also." Joanna had done that, and yet it's hard for us not to feel shocked by her radical leaving of her family. We realize that it's something we don't really expect anyone to do. Perhaps the male disciples did it, but a woman? Joanna heard Jesus and did exactly what he demanded: she left everything to follow him.

Joanna has been lost to us by neglect: which of us really wants to ponder a follower of Jesus who has truly forsaken all to follow him? It is time for us to reclaim her and consider what Joanna's radical discipleship might mean for us today.

In that early community, it is Joanna who, because of her education, background, and facility in both Greek and Aramaic, might have moved most easily between the Aramaic and Hellenistic communities. With her political savvy, she would have anticipated some of the conflicts within the early community.

And with her own experience of the radical nature of the gospel, Joanna would have been passionate that this extraordinary message not be watered down. She knew that all was demanded, and that old wineskins wouldn't work.

Because many of the issues threatening the earliest church would have been central for Joanna, we need to look at them before we can begin to find this amazing woman.

The Scene

Many of us imagine the early church as the one time when Christians got it right. Everything must have seemed so clear to those new believers. They shared everything, and they had long, charismatic services as a church completely unified and idyllic.

But in fact, when you read between the lines of the book of Acts, it is clear that there was a split between the Aramaic Jewish believers and the Hellenistic Jewish believers from near the church's beginnings. Huge issues were at stake: What does it mean to be a Christian? How is a person saved? What is Christianity—is it a whole new thing, or is it a variation on Judaism? This conflict is evident throughout the book of Acts and many of the epistles.

Language was central to this split, since table fellowship was at the center of the new faith. Aramaic was the language spoken in Judea and Galilee at the time of Jesus; the earliest followers of Jesus were mainly Aramaic-speaking. Jesus, James, Peter, and many of the women would have spoken Aramaic as their first language. Greek was a common language among these Hellenistic believers, and scholars speculate that Jesus spoke at least some Greek, as did many of the first followers of Jesus, but not as their first language. The one exception seems to have been Philip, who spoke Greek as his first language. (Remember in John's Gospel: Greeks come to Philip and say, "Sir, we would see Jesus.")

Aramaic-Speaking Believers

Not only did they speak a different language, but even after they believed in Jesus, many of these Aramaic-speaking believers saw themselves as a part of Judaism rather than a new religion. They saw their post-resurrection, post-Pentecost life with Jesus as a completion of Judaism (see notes, 99).

After all, the Jewish faith had been a great blessing to these Jews. They were God's chosen people, to whom God had given the law as a gift. Even after meeting Jesus, they kept the full Mosaic law, followed the rules regarding circumcision, and worshiped in the temple while praying and preaching Jesus. They saw themselves as Jews who had added a Messiah and Sunday table fellowship to their temple worship.

These early Aramaic Christians in Jerusalem were more conservative than Jesus had been, especially in terms of table purity (who you could eat with and what you might eat) as well as other aspects of the law. Some Pharisees became Christians but seem to have remained Pharisees in good standing. The Aramaic believers were led by James, the brother of Jesus, who was converted at the resurrection. Committed to Jewish practice, many of these believers would have regarded women in the light of contemporary commentary in the Mishnah. The "official Jerusalem teaching" Paul got about the resurrection— what he "received"—reflects this teaching by not mentioning the first witnesses as women, although all the Gospel accounts do.

These Aramaic believers, called "the Way," were generally well regarded by their fellow Jews but were seen as a bit eccentric. Until about 70 C.E., they remained a sect within Judaism. A person could understand themselves as a faithful member of Israel and a follower of Jesus at the same time.

Hellenistic Jewish Believers

On the other side of this split were the Hellenistic (Greek-speaking) Jewish believers (see notes, 100). Philip was typical of many other Hellenistic Jews of his day, who had grown up in other parts of the Roman Empire in Jewish communities centered in cities like Antioch and Alexandria. Many of these communities had synagogues and a Jewish community that met together. On the day of Pentecost, the different languages that the believers spoke were the local languages of Hellenistic Jews gathered for Pentecost in Jerusalem.

Hellenistic Jews not only spoke Greek as their first language, they are also thought to have been more cosmopolitan and perhaps a bit more liberal than their Aramaic-speaking counterparts. Throughout the empire, the Jewish faith was very attractive to people, with its monotheism and its demanding code of ethics. Many non-Jews became proselytes or God-fearers, associating with Hellenistic synagogues and worshiping God, though stopping short of circumcision. Hellenistic Jews had more contact with those outside the Jewish faith than did their Aramaic-speaking brethren.

Many Hellenistic Jews came to Jerusalem for the great Jewish festivals, and at that first Pentecost, it was these Hellenistic Jews who heard and responded to the new message. After Pentecost, they went to their home cities and preached the word. Scholars believe that by 40 c.e., there was a Christian community based on the synagogue in Rome and one created five or six years earlier in Damascus.

Other Hellenistic Jews had moved to Jerusalem to live, so that at the time of Jesus, there was a large community of Hellenistic Jews living in a separate part of Jerusalem. Many moved there to retire close to the temple, and a large number of the Hellenistic Jews in Jerusalem seem to have been widows who were dependent on the religious community (see notes, 101). One of the causes of conflict in the early church seems to have been that these Hellenistic widows had been unable to get food from the temple after they became Christians.

Living in Jerusalem must have been hard for many of these Jews who had lived in other parts of the empire. In their foreign homes, like Antioch or Alexandria, they were marginalized as Jews, and many thought that if they could live in the holy city, they would be full members of the community. But when they got to Jerusalem, they found that they were marginalized in a different way—they were Jews, yes, but they spoke Greek as their first language and held some views that set them apart from their Aramaic Jewish counterparts.

Perhaps it was this disappointment that led many Hellenistic Jews to be open to the message of Jesus. Hundreds of Hellenistic Jews responded that first day and took their message to other Hellenistic Jews in their Jerusalem neighborhood; soon there were thousands. Other Hellenistic Jews (including Saul) responded with outrage that the clear message of Judaism they had pursued to Jerusalem was being challenged by their own people. These were the ones who attacked Stephen.

By the time we meet Stephen in the beginning of Acts 6, there is a problem between the two groups, focused, according to Luke, on the distribution of food to widows, clearly emblematic of a deeper split (see notes, 101).

When Stephen and others are appointed as deacons, Luke tells us it is so that Peter and the others won't have to neglect the word of God to wait tables. But these chosen deacons were not table waiters; they were teachers, filled with the Spirit, recognized leaders of the Hellenistic Jewish believers.

The trouble Stephen stirs up is central to the controversy between Hellenistic and Aramaic-speaking believers. Although Stephen was the focus of the persecution, it must have been broader or the whole Hellenistic group would not have been scattered. The world stands on three things, according to a common saying in Judaism—the Torah, the temple, and good works—and Stephen spoke against them. The complaints against Stephen were that he spoke against Moses and God, that he "never stops speaking against this holy place and the law," and that he said, "Jesus of Nazareth will destroy this place and change the customs Moses handed on to us" (Acts 6:13-14).

The accusations against Stephen are confirmed in his sermon, which Luke quotes at length. What in this sermon, one that might put us to sleep, made his listeners furious? What we hear in this sermon is the difference in understanding between the Hellenistic and the Aramaic Jewish believers. Stephen is saying that the temple and the Torah are not very important, since God doesn't live in buildings made with hands. In his reference to a temple made with hands, Stephen is tactlessly comparing the Jewish temple to pagan idols. No, it is Jesus and the Spirit—that's what counts, according to Stephen. This is outrageous to his hearers, including the young Saul, who joins them in stoning him to death.

It's hard for us to imagine how radical this growing break was, and how deeply it shook Jewish identity as God's chosen people to whom God had given the Torah and the temple. For any Jew to move from that tradition to trusting Jesus and the Spirit was a shocking paradigm shift. God gives Peter visions and supernatural signs, but still he struggles to come to terms with this new way of thinking.

And so the early movement both attracted and repelled members through its amazing ideals: a loving Lord, the community as a family, and love for insiders and outsiders. The Christian attitude toward women, as well as Jesus' attitude to wealth, were simultaneously draws and stumbling blocks to outsiders.

The Hellenistic believers felt that the message of Jesus and the experience of the Spirit took precedent over Jewish tradition. During his earthly ministry, Jesus seems to have anticipated this broader scope of the gospel; he often applies Old Testament passages about the message going beyond the Jews to himself. He speaks to a Samaritan woman, to Roman soldiers, and to the Syrophoenician woman; he tells flattering stories about a Good Samaritan and non-Jews who were truer to the faith than God's chosen ones. Some scholars think that his understanding of his message and its scope may have been developing during his ministry, so that by the time Jesus cleanses the temple, he calls it "a house of prayer for all people." Before his ascension, Jesus sends believers out to Jerusalem, Judea, Sumaria, and the uttermost parts of the earth (Acts 1:8).

After Stephen's stoning, the split became physical, as "a severe persecution began against the church in Jerusalem, and all except the apostles were scattered" (Acts 8:1) It was a terrible persecution, and everyone was chased off except the apostles. The word *apostle* is used in a variety of ways in the New Testament, but most commonly as "one who is sent out with the message to plant new churches" (see notes, 102). And yet here the apostles are the ones who remain in Jerusalem, while the Hellenistic believers go out spreading the word and starting new churches.

So different were these two groups and their approaches to the new faith that the Aramaic Jewish believers were able to live unbothered in Jerusalem, acting as good Jews who happened to believe in the Messiah, while the Hellenistic believers were persecuted. The Aramaic Jewish Christians must have felt that the Hellenistic Jewish believers were being extreme, risking everyone's necks by being tactless. "You don't need to get yourself killed like that. Look at us. We're preaching daily, and people are getting saved—even some priests—so why go around rocking the boat on purpose? A nice guy, Stephen, but a bit of a fanatic."

Jerusalem, after the exit of the Hellenistic Jews, was peaceful (Acts 9:31), and perhaps more conservative without a dissenting element. The Hellenistic Christians took the word to the marginalized, and it seems significant that they went to the Samaritans (Acts 8:5), the hated enemies of the Jews, who argued against temple and Torah. Next Philip took the word to an Ethiopian eunuch who became the first non-Jewish convert to be baptized (Acts 8:27-39); Ethiopia was considered the extreme end of the world at this time, and eunuchs were outside the faith community, according to Jewish law.

Scholars argue that it was this—the scattering of a number of Greek-speaking believers—that allowed the new Christian message to spread throughout the Roman Empire (see notes, 101). Travel conditions were good, and Greek was the language of choice in the Roman world, so as new converts traveled, armed with the cherished words of their rabbi, the words of Jesus spread throughout the known world. Many of the Hellenistic Jewish missionaries were quite cosmopolitan. They not only spoke Greek but were familiar with Greek philosophy and began to use Greek ideas for theological terms. Although the ministry of Jesus was largely rural and local, Christianity soon became urban and international. Stephen's

message became central to the church's self-understanding: the life-giving Spirit's power, freedom, liberation, and the new creation.

As they took their message on the road, these Hellenistic Jewish believers found a ready audience among the many people who were attracted to the Jewish faith for its idea of a universal God, its focus on a high moral code, and its philanthropy. When hearers found that they could have the best of Judaism, minus the legalism, plus the gift of the Spirit, many converted.

This issue: what is Christianity—is it a whole new thing or a variation on Judaism?—was central in the early church.

Where were the women in this central controversy? It seems to me that the women would have been at the heart of this split, and that Joanna would have been key in working out these questions.

Found

Having rubbed shoulders with both the Aramaic-speaking and Greek-speaking believers, Joanna would have grasped clearly the complex and crucial nature of these issues in the infant church. And from her own life, Joanna was keenly aware of the radical nature of Jesus' call and the uselessness of trying to put new wine into old wineskins. Joanna's frustration with the conservatism of the Aramaic-speaking believers would have grown: the reaction of the Aramaic Christians to the death of Stephen was the last straw.

Joanna, you hold the key, sitting here, to the life of the early church. You are the one who can clearly see some of the fundamental issues in this formative time. You had to do what so many of us struggle to do: work out when to take a stand and not compromise, and when to allow for difference. Speak to us of your experience.

WHEN JESUS TOLD US that he was going away, we felt upset, yet we wanted to have faith . . . and I admit that I was afraid of what might happen to the movement. Jesus welcomed outsiders, bringing us into the inner circle, and I was afraid that the men might forget and slip back

into the old ways. It was hard to believe otherwise before Pentecost, with the men electing a substitute to the board of elders and making plans of various kinds. Martha was very encouraging. "It doesn't matter," she said. "We can trust Jesus."

And the gift of the Spirit seemed to fulfill that promise. Peter, especially, seemed to see that the Spirit was an indication of God's gift to all flesh, with daughters and sons dreaming prophetic dreams and spelling out visions. Perhaps Peter's new clarity convinced him that the religious establishment in Jerusalem would quickly recognize Jesus as Messiah, and then Jesus could return.

Sometimes in those early days I agreed with him, as thousands responded to the message, and I don't think any of us noticed at first who was responding—largely Hellenistic Jews from all over the empire but only a handful of the Aramaic-speaking religious leaders. Still, daily the men went to the temple to pray and preach, and it struck me pretty early on that the Jewish religious leaders had far too much to lose if they responded to this Messiah. Not only would they have to admit they were wrong, but they would have to say that Jesus and these Galilean peasants were right. Their grip on power was so strong. How could they loosen their grip on the power that was theirs through the law and their interpretation of it? They were on the inside track, seated right next to God himself.

And the idea of God becoming flesh, a God stripped naked, hanging on a cross, dying a slave's death—that was too much. When they thought about Jesus' own ministry, it was worse. Jesus on the side of tax collectors, sinners, and women? For them to turn to this Messiah would be like someone who thought they were holding the keys to the great city and then finding out that they were absolutely useless. People do not easily give up privilege and influence. It seemed to me a real long shot, the idea of all these men gladly relinquishing their power and bowing the knee to Jesus.

James, from his conversion after the resurrection, seemed like a prime example of what could happen to someone when they finally saw clearly. James became more of a leader, but he hadn't heard much of Jesus' teaching and hadn't heard him saying to the religious leaders, "Behold, tax collectors and sinners are going into the Kingdom before you."

In their efforts to win the Jewish establishment, the leadership of the Aramaic group felt we needed to be sensitive. Questions about the centrality of temple and Torah were not to be raised. Questionable people—Hellenistic Jewish believers and women—were asked to keep a low profile out of deference to the Jewish leaders who already had plenty to swallow in turning to Jesus. Jesus would come back soon, so it was for such a short time, and the whole of Jesus' life, death, and teaching—in fact, God's purpose—was at stake. Well, of course, put that way, it was hard to argue.

Then one day, Stephen and Philip asked Mary Magdalene and me if we would come to their Greek neighborhood and tell about Jesus— his life, death, and resurrection. Both of us had a sense of coming home. Instead of being anxious not to offend anyone, there was a sense of listening to the Spirit, wanting to follow Jesus, like what we'd known when we walked with Jesus. We started going to the Hellenistic quarter every day, and we finally moved there. I became a go-between, partly because of my fluency in Greek and Aramaic, but also because I was on close terms with some of the Aramaic followers. Many Greek-speaking widows, who had retired to Jerusalem to be near the temple, had become part of the Way. When they went to the temple to get their charitable food contributions, they were told that since they followed Jesus, they were no longer Jewish enough. More and more, the Hellenists saw their faith superseding Jewish law, and they relaxed their observance and went to the temple less and less.

The split was handled wisely, I thought, with the appointment of Hellenistic believers to lead that community, so that each could get on with what they felt called to do. Mary and I had long conversations with Stephen and the other leaders who were eager to know all Jesus had said about the temple and the law.

Stephen's death was horrible, but it was worse when we heard Aramaic believers talking about Stephen's fanaticism.

Stephen's sense of the meaning of the message was closer to mine. When I chose to follow Jesus, I left all: my home, my family, and all my *possessions. The idea of tinkering with your life, patching Jesus onto the old way—that is not what following Jesus is about. I don't regret my choice at all. . . .*

I had been unhappy for some time. Oh, life in Herod's court was glamorous and exciting, but Herod was becoming so deranged that you never knew what he would do next. Chuza and I had our own apart-ments in a different wing of the palace, but walking through the outer courtyard, we often passed scantily dressed women recently come from Herod's chambers. And then he clapped John the Baptist in prison. One morning, Chuza, looking very pale, told me how Herodias had bewitched Herod with her dancing the night before until he offered her anything, and she asked for John's head on a platter. I pleaded with Chuza to leave, but he wouldn't hear of it. And so I got on with life, sickened by some of what I saw, but delighted by the food, clothes, the excitement. . . .

I had heard rumors at palace dinners about Jesus, but once I crossed the square and realized he was there. I wanted to get close enough to hear him teach and see him heal someone. I imagined myself telling about it back at the palace. . . .

When I was close enough to hear him, a well-dressed young man stepped out of the crowd and spoke to Jesus. "Good teacher, what must I do to inherit eternal life?" By his accent, I could hear he was wellborn, and I realized he was one of the new rulers of the synagogue. Looking at him, I felt old, though in years I wasn't much older, but my years at the palace had made me worn and jaded.

"Good?" Jesus answered, moving closer. "Why are you calling me that when it is God who is good? What do you read in the scriptures?"

The young man looked down as he recited some of the com-mandments. Then he lifted his face to look at Jesus again, and I could see longing in his eyes. "But I've done these, all of them, since I was young."

I couldn't take my eyes off the face of this young man. He had wealth, youth, health, power, holiness, and a kind of desperation. Then I looked at Jesus' face. No wonder the young man was staring at him, open-mouthed. Jesus loved him, and our teacher's eyes seemed to act on the young man. Tears sprang to the young man's eyes.

"Go," Jesus said, in a voice that sounded like he was inviting him to a party. "Sell what you have and give it to the poor. And then come and join me."

"But . . ." he said, stepping back a pace and looking down. "I need to get back . . . my wife. My father . . ." He slipped through the crowd, and Jesus watched him until he was gone.

Those eyes, that invitation . . . it was not the kind of story for the palace. I slipped away, back toward my apartments. How could that young man have turned his back on meaning? For what? For a life of ease and comfort, and eventually boredom and death. . . . The scene haunted me for days. How could he have turned away? Perhaps he thought of his wife, of his children, of the people who depended on him in the synagogue, of his parents. But how could he have said no?

One night as I lay in bed after Chuza slept, seeing that face before my eyes, it hit me. I had walked away, too. I had turned my back. For what?

In the dark, the choice seemed enormous, and then it seemed like no choice at all. "Chuza. I cannot stay here anymore. I don't belong in this kind of place, this kind of life. I want to leave, and make a new life. Come with me." He threatened and pressured and finally asked me to leave. I packed a few belongings and joined the disciples who followed the Way.

I am still haunted by that young man's face. Sometimes I dream of him on his deathbed, tossing, saying, "Why, why, why, didn't I follow? I couldn't . . . my father . . . Lydia . . . and yet I've been so lonely, everlasting loneliness. No, no, let me choose again. No, I don't want any more wine, any sweets . . . they taste bitter to me. I want to follow. Love, love . . . how could I let it get away?" In the dream, I cannot comfort him. In turning away from that kind of love, his whole life has been interwoven with that loss. When I think of him, I know I made the right decision.

Jesus demands all and gives all. If the new way is worth following, it demands a new life. Stephen saw that and died for it. Mary and I will leave Jerusalem for the same reason.

Six

The Samaritan Woman

⁂

"IN ALL OF YOUR VOICES I hear the sound of living water. He gives us to drink, and the well does not run dry. I will never forget the day I met him." Suheir's accent and dress set her apart at this table (see notes, 103).

The hatred between Jew and Samaritan runs so deep that she cannot forget, nor can these other women, that this is the first time she has eaten with Jews and they with a Samaritan. If Martha's neighbor were to walk in, she would be shocked and revolted that a Samaritan woman sits here with Jewish women. Samaritan women were thought by Jews to be the depth of impurity, menstruants from the cradle, always and irretrievably ritually unclean (see notes, 103).

They can hardly believe that they are sitting here together, yet Jesus invited Suheir's discipleship several years before. And now the Hellenistic Jewish Christians, scattered after the death of Stephen, have gone to Samaria to preach, and word has come to Jerusalem of God's deliverance and healing. Those scattered believers must have been surprised to arrive in Samaria and find some who already believed in Jesus but knew nothing of his death and resurrection (see notes, 103).

Lost

The Samaritan woman occupies a key role in the Gospel of John; the passage about her takes up nearly a chapter, and she has been the topic of many sermons. In some ways she may be the least "lost" of these women, and yet it's easy to overlook the significance of her discipleship.

That Jesus talks to this woman is remarkable: his disciples are shocked, the Gospel tells us, to see Jesus talking to a woman. For Suheir to be at the well during the heat of the day meant she was avoiding the other village women who came early in the morning or in the evening, because she had kept a series of husbands and live-in lovers and was living with a man to whom she was not married. Jesus is speaking here with someone who as a Samaritan and a woman (and an immoral woman at that) was completely past praying for, beyond redemption.

Jesus' outrageousness to the religious establishment is encapsulated in his response to this woman. Suheir is the first person to whom Jesus reveals his true identity. "I who speak to you am he," says Jesus in response to her comment about the Messiah. Before any of the other disciples, before his mother, Jesus unmasks his crucial self to a Samaritan woman.

Suheir is the first non-Jew to become a follower of Jesus, and the first missionary, as she goes into her village telling about her encounter with Christ. The townsfolk, we are told, believe because of her word. Later in John, Jesus' high-priestly prayer is for his disciples and *those who will believe through their word*—the same phrase used of the Samaritan woman and those who hear her.

The first person to whom Jesus reveals his identity, the first non-Jewish follower, and the first missionary—Suheir is a mentor for us. When Jesus discusses this encounter with the male disciples, he tells them about the need to spread the message, because the fields are white for harvest. He speaks of one sowing and another reaping, clearly referring to the woman who went sowing, missionary-like, in her village so that others came out to meet Jesus. Suheir—a woman who is, by Jewish standards, the most unclean of the unclean—

becomes the first missionary/apostle, taking the word to her village and essentially founding a church there.

The great commission that Jesus gives before his ascension tells the followers that they will be his witnesses in Jerusalem, Judea, Samaria, and the uttermost parts of the earth. When Stephen is stoned and the Hellenistic believers scattered, they take Jesus' instructions to heart: Philip goes to Samaria for a highly successful mission. When we remember the issue with which the church in Jerusalem was struggling—the continuity of temple and Torah versus the revolutionary new way of the Spirit—Jesus' encounter with the Samaritan woman holds even greater significance. She brings up the question of the temple—you Jews say the temple is necessary, but we go for this mountain—and Jesus points to the deeper truth, that "true worshipers will worship in spirit and in truth." This is much closer to the attitude of the Hellenistic believers who left Jerusalem and arrived in Samaria. Add to this the Jewish hatred for the Samaritans, and it seems significant that the Hellenistic believers would go to those most hated by the Jewish authorities. In some ways, they seem to be shaking the Jerusalem dust off their feet and recognizing the utter newness of the mission of Jesus.

Samaria is a link between the Jewish church in Jerusalem and Judea and the burgeoning church in the rest of the world, a step on the way to the wider gentile mission. Suheir is the key, the one who stands between the Jewish mission and the gentile church. And at this table she also fulfills that role.

Suheir had indeed drunk the living water, finding her worship to be in spirit and truth. The first Christian missionary is a woman, a Samaritan, and someone with a painful and desperate past.

Found

Suheir smiles at the gathered group. "It is wonderful for me to hear about your encounters with the teacher. I see that this is indeed the same message that Jesus told me: the living water, springing up and up and up, is indeed the Spirit. We worship, and it doesn't matter where. This is the new wine, and we are the new wineskins. It is my joy to speak to you, because although you all know each other's stories, none of you have yet heard how I met him." She looks down at her hands and begins her story.

❧

WALKING TO THE WELL, lowering buckets, laboring back . . . morning and evening, day in, day out . . . women's work since the beginning of time. That day, in the midst of what is most ordinary, how could I know my life would be utterly transformed?

The loneliness . . . My village sisters stopped speaking to me, began staring at me; they believed I wanted to seduce their husbands or their sons. My shame was like my shadow on the walk to the well, until I could stand it no longer. I started making the long walk alone, sun beating down, muscles straining.

That day . . . I glanced up, and there was a man sitting in the shade. I could see he was Jewish, on his way to Jerusalem, I figured. I was an offense to his eyes. I knew that. I could not come here with the village women, because they know me and think me filth. I come in this heat, and here is a Jewish man who knows nothing of me, but considers me unclean from the cradle, because I am a woman of Samaria.

I'll come back later, I thought. Drawing water before the eyes of another who despised me . . . it overwhelmed me. But I was tired and desperately thirsty. I set down my jar. He was wondering what had brought me here at noon, thinking, I guessed, that I was the scum of the earth.

I listened for the sound of him spitting on the ground like a good Jewish man, in the presence of an obscenity like me. My shame rose before my eyes. I turned my back. I would get my water and get away as fast as I could.

And then I heard a voice, his voice. "Give me a drink," he said.

I was prepared for him to spit, to cover his face . . . but to speak to me?

"You, a Jew, ask me, a Samaritan, for a drink?" He knew as well as I did that if I gave him water he would be polluted.

I turned to hear his answer. He said that if I could catch a glimpse of the gift God wanted to give me, if I could see for a moment who was asking me, then I would have asked him for a drink. And he would have given me water, living water.

Me, ask a Jewish man for water? If I were dying of thirst, I could not. . . .

Yet here was this man talking about giving me a drink. "You don't have a bucket," I finally said. I told him the well was deep, built by Jacob. Then I looked into his face.

What he said . . . was wonderful. He talked of our deep human thirst. About coming every day to the well and how the water quenches but only for a few hours. And back we come with our empty buckets.

Then he spoke about his water, which would quench a person's deepest thirst, until it became a fountain deep within, a spring that bubbled always. Then he was silent.

I wanted to hear his voice again, and oh how I wanted the water he spoke about. "Give me that water," I said. "Please, please, sir. I'm so weary of coming here, of getting thirsty all the time, of never being deeply satisfied. Please."

He listened, and then he looked into my face. "Go," he said, "and call your husband."

Shame rushed over me. No more blood, but shame pulsing through every vein. Oh, I'd known it was too good to be true. A Samaritan, a woman—filthy enough, but anyone who knew, who really knew me . . .

Living water evaporated like a mirage, gone, vanished. Overwhelming regret, grief welled up from my deepest being. I would fight not to lose this. "I don't have a husband," I said, looking down. The silence pressed on me, pounded in my ears.

Finally he spoke. "I guess that's true," he said, and I looked up at him. He shook his head. "You've had five husbands, and the one you are with now is not your husband." My burning shame froze throughout my body. How could this Jewish man, a stranger here, how could he know my life?

I was terrified. All I'd feared about God—a God who knew my deepest secrets, the deeds I'd done in private . . . I wanted to run away, but you could not hide from this nightmarish God. I felt hunted, cornered. He knew. . . .

I looked up. And saw compassion. My life was very sad, his face said, tragic . . . like, I don't know, like news of a drought. . . . But there was no condemnation, just sorrow. . . .

"You seem to be a prophet," I heard myself saying. And my terror of God was washed over by desire, a longing to know what this God was like, the one whom I had feared and doubted and longed for. I was desperate to know, and yet all I could think of was the question I'd overheard in countless religious discussions, the age-old Jewish/Samaritan question: should we worship in Jerusalem or on Mount Gerezim?

He looked searchingly at me before he spoke, and his answer cut through those endless theological quarrels. His words etched themselves forever on my mind: The time is coming, he said, when worshiping in Jerusalem or on Mt. Gerezim . . . it won't matter. The time is coming . . . in fact, he said, it is here now, and those who seek God, who worship God, will worship in spirit and truth. Those are the worshipers God wants. God . . . remember . . . is Spirit, not stone, not wood, and real worship is in spirit and truth.

What was he saying? He was talking about the future and the now as if they were coming together, as if at this moment, by this well, eternity had entered now. God here, God now . . . I felt dizzy . . . and I thought of the Messiah—the anointed one who I knew was meant to bring God's rule. "I know the Messiah is coming," I said. "And when the Messiah comes, everything will be clear."

And then he said it. He said it. "I who speak to you. I am he."

I stood, water jar at my side, and I knew it was true. I had met the Messiah. I was standing on the holiest of holy ground. Me talking to the Messiah . . . but it was more than that . . . the Messiah talking to me. What kind of Messiah was this? He knew I was a Samaritan, a woman. He knew my deepest, darkest secrets—and yet Messiah was speaking to me, offering me living water. I looked into his face, and my tears overflowed.

Before I could collect myself, I heard voices. . . . It was some of his disciples, and I couldn't look at them. I heard a couple of whispers:

"What will he do next . . . talking to a Samaritan woman?" "What's she doing out here this time of day?" I looked up to see Jesus silencing them with a stare. He looked at me, and then he smiled.

And I felt I was going to burst with excitement; I dropped my jar against the fountain and ran toward the village.

When I got there, people started leaning out their windows, coming out of their houses. I'm not sure what it was—perhaps the sight of a woman running in the heat of the day. "Listen," I said. "I have just met . . . the most amazing . . . Jewish man out at the well. He talked to me, and he knew about my whole life. He's got the truth. I think this is the Messiah. . . . Come with me, let's go catch him and get him to stay."

People said to me afterwards that the change in my face, my voice, my eyes—it was so compelling that they followed me. I had never felt so happy. . . . Here I was, most unclean of the unclean, leading a group of my townsfolk through the blazing noonday sun. I wanted to dance and shout, so great was my joy.

When we got to the well, Jesus nodded and smiled at me as if we were old friends. People looked at Jesus and glanced at me. Someone asked him if he would stay a few days, and then everyone took up the request. He taught and healed. My life was changed forever. . . .

A couple of weeks ago, Philip arrived in our little town and started preaching about Jesus. He was surprised when a number of us said, "Yes, we are followers of this Jesus Messiah."

After my baptism, it was clear to me that I should come to Jerusalem to meet some of the eyewitnesses, to hear more of Jesus' teachings, and learn more of his death and resurrection. Philip told me to come here, to this house in Bethany. He warned me that some of the followers here in Jerusalem might be unhappy that believers were taking the message to Samaria, since they felt the message was for Jews only. And when I told him my story, he said they might not be pleased that Jesus himself had taken the message to our village.

Bless God with me, my sisters. I was lonely, ostracized from my village and from my sisters there. All I had was my shame. But from that first sip of living water, I was given a message. I took it to my village. Where else I will take it I do not know. But here I sit with you, my sisters, lonely and ashamed no more. Praise be to Jesus.

Seven

Martha

❧

"WELCOME TO THIS TABLE, THIS FEAST," says Martha to Suheir and to all of us. "Jesus has called me to welcome you."

We know Martha's name, but Martha, the strong follower of Jesus, has been lost to us (see notes, 104). Her loss is different from that of Mary Magdalene or Joanna. Mentioned a number of times in Scripture, biblical interpretation and societal attitudes toward women have intertwined to trivialize Martha's life and witness. She has come to embody the little woman who fusses about her house and her meals, as women do, God bless them!

Sitting here at this table, I would like to reintroduce Martha, not as a trivial little woman, but as an energetic and gifted woman of faith who needed the encouragement of the rabbi so that she could use her gifts. In many ways, Martha is truly the mentor, the model to contemporary women.

Martha and her sister lived in Bethany together with their brother Lazarus, the one whom Jesus raised from the dead. Jesus stayed with them regularly when he came to Jerusalem for festivals, and Bethany was perhaps the place most like home for him. When the three siblings are mentioned, Martha is listed first: scholars conclude that Martha had become most prominent in the Christian communities into which the Gospels were written. John writes that "Jesus loved Martha and her sister and Lazarus" (11:5), a phrase that he otherwise reserves for himself as "the disciple whom Jesus loved."

In Luke's Gospel, we are told the wonderful story of Martha going to Jesus and asking him to get Maria to help her fix supper. Jesus' response—telling Martha that Maria, in sitting and listening and learning from a rabbi, is doing the better part—may not seem that remarkable to us as we read the story. But it was radical at the time, when Martha was doing what a good woman should, and Maria wasn't.

Jesus says that Maria's discipleship and her learning from a rabbi are what truly count. Given the societal pressures against women's full involvement in religious life, Jesus was offering these women a radical alternative. Respectable women in first-century Judaism and society were told that they should not be seen in public, should not speak to a man in public, could not be taught the Torah, and could never follow a rabbi; they could not make ethical decisions without the supervision of a father or husband. Jesus makes no distinction between male and female followers—all are called to listen, learn, grow, and follow.

Lost

Luke recorded this scene some thirty years after it happened, and its presence in the Gospel should count as one of the biggest miracles of all time. The Gospel writers mention the difficulty of selection so that their written accounts don't run into thousands of pages, and yet Luke includes here a domestic scene: no dead raised or demonized delivered, but a scene of domestic priority finding. It is a scene that speaks with a prophetic voice against the culture of the time, saying that Jesus cares about women followers as much as about men, that the rabbi doesn't want women's lives trivialized.

Although Jesus' words to Martha, recorded by Luke, are unequivocal, they have scattered, making little impression on dominant understandings of what women should be. Dorothy L. Sayers points out in her essay "The-Human-Not-Quite-So-Human" that it is hard to find a preacher who takes the words of Jesus seriously:

> I have never heard a sermon preached on the story of Martha and Mary [Maria] that did not attempt, somehow, somewhere, to explain away its text. Mary's, of course, was the better part—the Lord said so and we must not precisely contradict Him. But we will be careful not to despise Martha. No doubt, He approved of her too. We could not get on without her, and indeed (having paid lip service to God's opinion) we must admit that we greatly prefer her. For Martha was doing a really feminine job, whereas Mary [Maria] was just behaving like any other disciple, male or female; and that is a hard pill to swallow.

Even the clearest words of Jesus diffuse when they meet a strong societal thrust in the opposite direction. Similarly, we miss the strength of Martha in her encounters with Jesus in the book of John. We see Martha fussing, this time because her brother Lazarus has died. A few chapters later, there she is serving at table again. Will she ever quit? Martha is sweet, yes, but rather trivial.

And so Martha has come to epitomize the women who busies herself, without being contemplative or mystical like her sister. As this person of action, Martha stands as the type of the contemporary Western Christian who "just does it" without spending too much time reflecting.

Anyone can be given to action like Martha. The poison of action as it has been associated with Martha is that it has become an ideal: the perfect little woman who does and does, always for others and without asking questions, until the day she dies. This ideal "Martha" runs the church bake sales and rummage sales. Dorothy L. Sayers used to say that a bored woman was a dangerous woman: all that God-given energy channeled into housekeeping becomes obsessive and damaging to the woman and those around her. If Martha had not listened to Jesus, she might have become dangerous.

Martha did listen to Jesus, and so becomes for contemporary women a model of listening to Christ to find what we are called to do. And yet, we might puzzle that Martha seems to disappear at the end of the Gospels, never to be seen again. Did Martha decide (since Jesus had ascended) that she would open a bed and breakfast?

(Seems like she could have had some interesting plaques on the walls: Jesus sat here. Jesus slept here.)

How can we begin to trace this missing person, to find the real Martha?

Martha did not disappear; she took an active leadership role in the early church, leading a house meeting in her home. The words of Jesus were treasured in the early church, and Martha was one of the best sources, a valued teacher and evangelist. In fact, Martha was fortunate. She was one of the few alive at the perfect moment when she (as a woman) was encouraged to be a true follower, using her gifts for the rabbi. Thousands of years before and after, Martha would have been squelched, told to limit herself because she was female.

Looking at John's Gospel, written around the year 90 c.e., we see more of Martha and the key role she played in the Johannine community. Martha must have followed Jesus' advice to choose the better part, because we see her at the death of her brother Lazarus voicing the great words of faith to Jesus: "I believe that you are the Christ, the Messiah" (John 11:27), the great statement of faith Peter voices in the other Gospels. (And on the strength of that, Peter is seen as founder and first pope of the church. What does that make Martha?)

By the time John's Gospel was written, Martha was clearly a leader in the church. In John 12:2, she is said to serve at table (*diakonein*). This word, translated "to serve" had become, by the time John wrote his Gospel, a technical term for someone who presided at the eucharistic agape feast: to fulfill the office of *diakonos*, a person was ordained through the laying on of hands, which made the church's stamp of approval official. Martha was not the only woman who did this, but she was certainly one who was ordained in this way.

No, Martha is not lost. She was an active, "ordained" member of the Johannine community, known for her outspoken prophetic words and her role in presiding at the table. Having chosen the better part, Martha followed Jesus after his death as a leader in the church.

Found

The image of Martha as *diakonos*—standing, holding up the bread, and blessing it to be God's food for her gathered house church—stands before us as we consider Martha. The table is central to Martha. Before her encounter with Jesus, the table was central, because that was where she tried to prove herself worthy. Her life and the table are transformed as she finds her calling in Jesus.

Martha's calling centers on the table, just as during the life of Jesus and the fledgling church, the table took center stage. Clean and unclean foods, ritual slaughter, fear of contamination, ritual purity—these were all table issues, key to Jewish self-identification (see notes, 104). Jesus was criticized for not washing properly before meals and for eating with those he should not have eaten with: tax collectors and sinners. Over and over in the Gospels, Jesus sits at table with people, eating, drinking, and talking.

At table, Jesus is anointed by a sinful woman in the presence of some Pharisees (a scene that Frend argues probably led to their decision that Jesus needed to be killed). At table, you get the working out of Zacchaeus's repentance; at table, Maria anoints Jesus for his death. At the Last Supper, Jesus fills the table fellowship/Passover meal with special significance. The disciples on the road to Emmaus recognize Jesus when he breaks bread with them at table.

The table became central to the young Christian movement; besides a belief in Jesus as Messiah, the new believers were distinguished from nonbelieving neighbors by a weekly fellowship meal, a continuation of the table fellowship that Jesus instituted, held on the first day of the week.

Table purity became a central issue in the new movement. When God is trying to get through to Peter about welcoming gentiles to the faith, Peter sees a vision of clean and unclean food. At one point in his ministry, Peter comes to Jerusalem and eats with non-Jews. James and others complain, and he changes his policy. In the Jerusalem council, table purity is a central issue: whom do you allow to eat with you, and what do you eat? The church in Antioch struggled over who could sit at table together.

As discussed, the earliest church in Jerusalem was divided into two groups. Some scholars argue that women presiding at table fellowship may well have been a factor in this split between the Hellenistic Jewish believers and the Aramaic believers. The more cosmopolitan Hellenistic believers were used to the idea of women presiding at table fellowship, since Greek women took leading roles in cultic worship. Those who saw themselves as a sect of Judaism would have been less comfortable with female leadership (see noes, 105).

If this was an issue in the early Jerusalem church, Martha would have been caught in the middle. She was Aramaic-speaking, but I suspect Martha's encounters with the liberating Jesus may have clinched for her a sense of calling that she was unwilling to let go, despite societal pressures. And because of her special place in the heart of Jesus, as "one whom Jesus loved," the Aramaic-speaking believers would have been unable to hobble Martha and her ministry.

Martha welcomed a gathering on that first day of the week, presiding at the house meeting. Here she could bring together gifts of hospitality and leadership. Valued by the early church as one who walked with Jesus, she was an invaluable source of Jesus sayings. Their home, I suspect, was often visited by outsiders wanting to meet eyewitnesses and hear Jesus stories.

Martha looks at the wine in front of her and then around the table. She speaks.

₰

I HAVE BEEN CALLED by Jesus to welcome you all to this table, to bring you together here. Filled with the Spirit, I am both the same and a very different person than the one who met Jesus those years ago. That woman, who came into this room to complain to Jesus about my lazy sister, that woman was me, but warped as you are when you don't have peace and a strong sense of inner call.

That woman was the same, and yet she was the opposite. Then I needed to hear people praise my home, my cooking, my efficiency, all voices from the outside. The call from God wells up from within, linking my gifts and what I care most deeply about. I don't use it to feed me, but instead to follow: that is how God has chosen to work in the world.

The call of God springs directly out of the love of Jesus, poured out on us in the Spirit. It was as if that dance with God, the dance of my deep joy, flowed into the church's need; the fellowship was blessed, and I was blessed. As we started having our house meetings on the first day of the week to commemorate Jesus' resurrection, I started having one here, of course, and it was wonderful. It seemed like Jesus was here just as he had been then, but because he wasn't physically present, he said, "Go ahead, Martha, you serve. You be my hands, my voice." I served as I had; I reminded people of how he had eaten with us so many times in his life, and how he was present eating with us now.

We got into the habit of saying Jesus' own words from that last night, and we knew that we were being fed by the presence of Jesus in our midst.

After a couple of years, James and Peter came over one evening, and I could see they had something on their minds. They started talking about not wanting to upset any of the people that they were trying to evangelize, some of whom were fairly conservative. . . . I couldn't understand what they were getting at until it hit me that they were talking about my presiding at the table fellowship. "You expect me to disobey the risen Jesus, present in the Spirit, so that you won't upset people?" I laughed aloud.

There is no question that we were called to full partnership, and that there can be no going back. I wanted to say to Peter and James, "So you want me to be circumcised, too?" But I thought I'd leave them to figure out that the old wineskins weren't going to hold the new wine.

This calling is so much a part of who I am that I can't imagine not following it. And I believe that this table must be open. I am rejoicing that Suheir is here with us tonight. It is right that all those whom Jesus loves and calls should gather together.

My hope is that Jesus will come again soon, and I will never see the day when I'm asked to stop following Jesus' call to me.

Eight

The Meeting

✤

"NOW IS THE TIME FOR THE BANQUET." For that which was lost has been found," says Martha, her hand on the cup of wine as she looks around the gathered faces. "'This is my blood,' Jesus said. We gather here on this first day of the week, the day our sorrow was changed to joy. This day is holy, because it changed the world forever. Do you remember? We thought that all was over, that the vision of a community of love and healing had all been a dream, that the idea of God walking amongst us had been a hopeless fantasy. . . . And then Mary Magdalene walked in this door. 'I have seen the Lord,' she said. What we share now, and what we have shared here of our stories: all is possible because of that day. Just as he changed water to wine at Cana, he has forever changed our lives."

She holds up the cup of wine. "'This is my blood,' Jesus said, because there is no time when Jesus is not with us. That is what we share here. Instead of shame and loneliness, Suheir has found love and borne fruit; and so have we all. Mary has seen the Lord alive. That was her message to us and will be her message as she goes beyond Jerusalem; it is our message, too. Joanna has known the faithfulness of God from that first day when she decided to follow Jesus, and so have we all. Maria has been filled with the Spirit since that day of Pentecost, just as we have all drunk of that same Spirit. Mary, mother of Jesus, has known herself called as follower and collaborator with God; so have we. Susannah has known God's faithfulness into her days of gray hair: God is faithful to each of us. And I have known the call of God in my life, just as you have, a call from which I can never walk away. Jesus has given all of us to drink of his new wine, his new covenant."

Looking around the table, Martha lifts her voice and sings:

> *God our beloved,*
> *who alone can receive*
> *the enormity of our love;*
> *you embrace our yearning*
> *and are not overwhelmed by our need.*
> *Let us love you with all that we are,*
> *and stretch us wider still.*

"Whether we stay here in Jerusalem or take the message beyond, whether we forsake all that we know or stay with what is known, we belong to Jesus," Martha continues. "We have experienced him in the flesh, his presence in the Spirit, his call to be a loving family. We are one, even with those who are not here, our sisters—Salome, Lydia, Rhoda—and with those who will come after us. With them we share this cup, and with our friend and mentor Jesus.

"Drink this and remember."

They slowly pass the cup, Martha begins singing a psalm, and soon the other voices join hers:

> *From the deep places of my soul I praise you, O God:*
> *I lift up my heart and glorify your holy name.*
> *From the deep places of my soul I praise you, O God:*
> *how can I forget all your goodness towards me?*
> *You forgive all my sin, you heal all my weakness,*
> *you rescue me from the brink of disaster,*
> *you crown me with mercy and compassion.*
> *You satisfy my being with good things,*
> *so that my youth is renewed like an eagle's.*
> *You fulfill all that you promise,*
> *justice for all the oppressed.*

Mary Magdalene has begun weeping softly. "I know that God is faithful, but it is hard to leave this place. We have known so much joy and pain here in Jerusalem, at Bethany. I know Jesus will go with us by his Spirit. . . . But could we be making a mistake? Pray for us, sisters."

"We need your confirmation," Joanna says. "Barnabas and Philip feel very clear that some of us who have been witnesses and know the Jesus words and stories must go beyond Jerusalem to share with the new believers. But James and the others argue that the message belongs in the holy city, that Jesus will come back to Jerusalem. And Peter is so confused; he and John are going in the next few days to visit the church at Samaria, and I'm sure he'll rejoice. But one minute he's talking about the beloved Jewish traditions and the next about the Spirit's new work. . . ."

Martha nods and bows her head. They all sit quietly.

After a few minutes, Martha looks up. "Suheir is your answer: God once again speaking in flesh and blood. Suheir came to us wanting to hear our words, and yet, sitting here, she is a word to you: Jesus met her while she was distant. She is why you will go to Antioch and perhaps beyond. There are many like her who never had the chance to meet Jesus in the flesh. You will be the incarnate word to them, as Suheir has been to you."

Suheir looks up and smiles, tears in her eyes. "Think of them, all those thirsty ones. The living water flows; it cannot be stopped. God visited me, despised and ashamed. Think of the others. Let me sing a song for you:

> *Tender God,*
> *you have seen my affliction,*
> *and unbound my eyes;*
> *you have bereaved me of the burden*
> *to which I used to cling;*
> *you have woven my pain*
> *into patterns of integrity;*
> *the wounds I cherished*
> *you have turned into honors,*

and the scars I kept hidden
into marks of truth.
You have touched me gently;
I have seen your face, and live.

Suheir looks around the table. "Many others will see his face, will find their wounds healed, because you go," she finishes.

They sit for a little longer, and then Mary speaks. "What comes to me is another song from when I took Jesus—he was tiny—to the temple. I wonder if the song of old Simeon is not for you today. . . ."

Praise be to God, that I have lived to see this day,
God's promise is fulfilled, and my duty done.
At last you have given me peace,
for I have seen with my own eyes
the salvation you have prepared for all nations
a light to the world in its darkness,
and the glory of your people Israel.

"Prepared for all nations . . ." Joanna murmurs.

Mary Magdalene looks up: "A light to the world in its darkness."

The women sit quietly for a few more minutes. "I think this is the time, Maria, for you to tell us more of your visions," Martha says.

"Yes, this is the time." Maria looks at the table in front of her. "I see hundreds of people who are followers of the Way. Many are people I've never seen before: very dark or with long yellowish, whitish hair, people with dark skin and straight black hair. I know when I see them that they are singing about Jesus; they are filled with the same Spirit. . . .

"I've seen wonderful sights: people, in the name of Jesus, caring for the sick, thousands of sick, but the followers of Jesus are tending them. Or people who are desperately afraid, who need to be hidden, and believers are helping them at great risk to their own lives. In one dream, a group of people black, white, and brown pray and pray together, arms around each other. Large gatherings, small gatherings. Thousands of people speaking in languages I cannot understand, but I know they are praising him." She pauses.

"We say Maranatha," says Martha. "Wanting Jesus to come back and make everything right. But I am beginning to believe, with Maria's visions and your calling to go beyond the holy city, that it might be many years before the end."

"It is right that you should go, that we send you from us to take the words of Jesus to the rest of the world. I've seen it clearly. You must go." Maria nods to them, and then her eyes fill with tears.

All the women sit quietly.

"What do you see that makes you weep, Maria?" Mary Magdalene breaks the silence. "Please tell us. This is too heavy for you to carry alone."

Maria's eyes overflow. "Some of what I see is terrible. I see people doing horrors in the name of Jesus, hurting, even killing people, fighting wars. . . ." She shakes her head as if to dispel the images. "How could it happen?" She sits for a minute and then wipes her eyes and speaks again.

"And in many of the visions, it is as if there are no women left on earth or in the church. There are no women, or the women are silent. . . . And in some, men are speaking, saying horrible things about women being the devil's gateway, questioning whether or not women have souls. But then I think it's impossible, Jesus wouldn't allow it. . . ." The women look into each other's faces.

"And then there are images that haunt me . . . over and over, pictures of a woman bent over, kneeling before an angel, over and over . . . a woman weeping for her sins, weeping and weeping. . . .

"Or I see worshipers gathered in an enormous building, very dark except for the most beautiful light coming from openings high above, blue like moon light, and other colors, red and yellow. It is lovely . . . but then I see that the worshipers are clustered around a doll with a crown. They are lighting candles, and I cannot see what this means about these believers. . . ."

Maria covers her face with her hands. "Jesus wouldn't let that happen. . . ."

The women sit, a few softly weeping. Several minutes pass before Mary Magdalene speaks.

"All we can really know is that God is good, and we are with Jesus. That is all we have known from the beginning when we walked with Jesus, even when he was killed and brought back to life; it is all we know now."

"All we can do is to follow our good Master," Martha agrees. "That is what God has given us to do. Here in Jerusalem, in Galilee, in Antioch, in Rome, perhaps . . . it is all the same."

"We have freedom in Jesus and the Spirit," Joanna says. "And we follow wherever we are called. We are with Jesus, and with each other by the Spirit."

"Yes," Mary Magdalene speaks again. "The Spirit breathes that message of love in our hearts, and we listen and follow. No matter what happens, the light shines in the darkness, and the darkness cannot overpower it."

Mary, mother of Jesus, stands and holds her hands out so that all the women move. She begins to sing the song, given to her when she carried the Messiah within, a song that by this time was already being sung in the church. The other women join her as they gather around Mary Magdalene and Joanna, encompassing them with their prayers:

> *Sing out, my soul,*
> *sing of the holiness of God:*
> *who has delighted in a woman,*
> *lifted up the poor,*
> *satisfied the hungry,*
> *given voice to the silenced,*
> *grounded the oppressor,*
> *blessed the full-bellied with emptiness,*
> *and with the gift of tears*
> *those who have never wept;*
> *who has desired the darkness of the womb,*
> *and inhabited our flesh.*
> *Sing of the longing of God,*
> *sing out, my soul.*

In the center of this circle of faith, the two women feel the hands of their sisters on them, hear the quiet murmuring of their sending prayers.

Finally, Martha speaks a blessing over them:

> *May the God who shakes heaven*
> *and earth,*
> *whom death could not contain,*
> *who lives to disturb and heal us,*
> *bless you with power to go forth*
> *and proclaim the gospel. Amen.*

Questions for Individual and Group Study

❧

IF A GROUP IS GOING TO STUDY THIS BOOK, my suggestion is that they read the preface, the prologue, and chapter 1 for the first meeting, then begin by discussing these questions. Before the next meeting, they should read the relevant chapter and do the individual questions. Group study questions in subsequent weeks will draw on the individual study questions.

Prologue and Chapter 1: Lost and Found at the Table

1. What has been your impression of the women in the New Testament, and where does it come from (flannel board illustrations, Bible art, stories, churches)? Go around the group, and have each person share an answer to this question. Have one person record common and distinct ideas from the group and summarize them after everyone has spoken.

2. How should we, as women today, react to the "lostness" of these great women of faith? Should we be mad, leave the church in droves, be sad, strive to correct this, or accept it as our cross to bear?

3. It's hard for us to imagine the earliest church, when new believers met together. Pretend that your group is a house meeting of the earliest Christians in Jerusalem—three years after Jesus' death and resurrection—much like the women meeting in *Spirited Women*.

   a. What would be the same for those women and your group? List some similarities.

   b. What would have been different? (This can be hard, but think about Judaism, their expectations of the Messiah, the lack of a New Testament, the limited geographical area, and so forth.)

4. If, as many of us say every Sunday in the creed, we believe in the "communion of saints," we can feel connected with people of faith who have gone before us. Read Hebrews 12:1-2 aloud. Here the writer of the letter to the Hebrews is writing about a crowd who is cheering us on, those who are our forefathers and mothers in the faith. What kind of connection do you feel to these foremothers of the faith?

5. Before you finish, talk together about your expectations for your group meetings, and pray together.

Chapter 2: Mary Magdalene

Individual Study Questions

Slowly read through some of the biblical passages that include references to Mary Magdalene (Luke 8:1-3; 23:46-12; Matthew 27:55-28; Mark 15:40—16:11; John 19:25; 20:1-18). Then consider these questions, drawing from your own life experience, the passages, the background, and Mary Magdalene's story in chapter 2. You may find it helpful to write down some of your responses in a journal.

1. Although we are given little information about Mary Magdalene, it seems she must have been an extraordinary person to have been so close to Jesus and to have been in the center of so many of the key moments in the Gospels. What qualities do you see in her? Which of these would you like to emulate?

2. Most qualities have two sides: one is a strength, and the other is its shadow, a vulnerability or a weakness.

> a. What do you think are some of the strengths/weaknesses in Mary Magdalene? (For example, if she was very sensitive, what strengths and weaknesses might have emerged from that quality?)
>
> b. What qualities do you have that make you vulnerable, but at the same time could be considered (or might become) strengths?

3. Mary Magdalene was given a message to take to the other disciples, and they considered it idle chatter. Have you had the experience of feeling like you had a message that was discounted or ignored? How have you handled feeling that way? What is the best way to handle that kind of situation?

4. For a woman, to go to the cross or the tomb of a crucified criminal was known to be dangerous. Mary Magdalene and the other women would have known this. What gave Mary Magdalene the courage to go to these places?

5. Why do you think Jesus chose Mary Magdalene to be the first witness to the resurrection? What does it mean to you that the first witness was a woman?

6. Why was the whole experience of Jesus' death and resurrection so different for the women and the men? What can you learn from this difference?

Group Study Questions

1. Share your impressions of Mary Magdalene that you noted in questions 1 and 2 in the individual study questions. How much do you find yourselves in agreement as a group on the kind of person she was (and on her strengths and weaknesses)?

2. Mary Magdalene should inspire us to cultivate our vulnerabilities and allow them to become strengths. Share with the group the

parallels in your own life that you noted in question 2b of the individual study questions: for example, areas that are weaknesses, but also indications of strengths, like Mary Magdalene had.

3. People have tried to account for Mary Magdalene's closeness to Jesus, often in ways that sexualize their relationship. Although these people seem to think they're being very radical, it seems to me not unlike what Augustine and Aquinas argued about God introducing Eve in the garden of Eden: that it must have been for sex, or why wouldn't God have just provided a man, since they are clearly so much better company than women? What do you think of Mary Magdalene's closeness with Jesus? What was it about? Share with the group some of your answers to questions 4 and 5 in the individual study questions. Why was she there at the cross and the tomb? Why was she the first witness?

4. Many branches of the church still consider the words of women to be "idle chatter." Drawing on your answers to question 3 in the individual study questions, what do you think can be done about that?

5. When you consider what the church has done with Mary Magdalene down the ages, it's easy to see a lot of fear and revulsion. Why do you think portraying Mary Magdalene as a fallen woman created a level of safety for the church?

> a. One thing that seems clear from the sad history of Mary Magdalene's treatment by the church is just how vulnerable we are to cultural biases entering and warping our theological understandings. Are there ways that we can try to protect ourselves from this? What are some areas that the church is warping at the beginning of a new millennium?

6. What is Mary Magdalene's message for us as women in the church today? How can we be involved in helping the church reclaim this wonderful, inspiring woman?

Chapter 3: Maria, Sister of Martha

Individual Study Questions

Read slowly through some of the biblical passages that include references to Maria (Luke 10:38-42; John 11:1-44; 12:1-8; Matthew 26:6-13). Then consider these questions, drawing from your own life experience, the passages, the background, and Maria's story in chapter 3. You may find it helpful to write down some of your responses in a journal.

1. In Luke 10, Maria is extraordinary in the way she resists doing what is expected of her as a woman. What do you think gave her the strength to resist getting up and getting busy? Would you say that this strength is some sort of innate personality trait, something she grew into, or a part of her newfound strength in Christ? Is it all of the above, or something else? How much of our strength comes from these sources?

2. Jesus says this about Maria to her sister: "Maria has made the better choice, which will not be taken away from her." If Jesus were to speak about you as he spoke about Maria here, what might he say about your choices? Are your priorities ones that he would rave about? Would he say they are a bit of a mixture? Or might he regard them as he seems to regard Martha's, as distractions?

3. The strength Maria shows in Luke 10 is radically countercultural: how do you see that strength played out in the other places this woman is shown in the Gospels (see John 11; 12.)?

4. When Jesus hears Lazarus is sick, the gospel says he loves Lazarus and his sisters; therefore, he doesn't buzz immediately over to help them. I've always thought, With friends like that. . . .

   a. Have you had experiences of waiting that have (in retrospect) seemed like times of great learning?

   b. What might that experience—Jesus not coming when she wanted him to, and then raising her brother from the dead—have meant to Maria in her ongoing life of faith?

5. In the parallel passages of John 12 and Matthew 26, Maria seems to make an almost inappropriate emotional, intimate scene. It seems as if it's embarrassing, and some people there mutter about it. Have you been criticized for following a spontaneous whim? Have there been times when you didn't, but you wished you had?

6. Jesus says (in Matthew 26:13) that "wherever this good news is proclaimed in the whole world, what she has done will be told in remembrance of her." This reaction seems a little much; she's only anointed him. How do you understand the strength of Jesus' reaction to this action?

7. In Acts 2, we are told about the day of Pentecost and the gift of the Spirit, which seemed to change everything for these new believers. Have you ever had an experience of God that was not (presumably) like the one Maria had, but one that seemed to you to speak of God's presence?

Group Discussion Questions

1. What are some of the pressures you feel? To perform to a certain societal standard, to be a good woman, a good mother, and a good Christian? Have things changed much since Maria's time?

2. Looking at Maria's strength in defying societal pressures—to help her sister in the kitchen, to not do "unwomanly" things like listening to a rabbi, to not be publicly emotional—how did she do these things? Share some of your answers from question 1 in the individual study questions: was she just that kind of person, or was there something else going on here?

3. So often it is in tough times, in times of loss and waiting, that we grow most. Using your answers from question 4 in the individual study questions, consider how that was true for Maria and has been true for you.

4. What is the big deal here? Why does Jesus say that whenever the gospel is preached, this will be told in memory of her? Share your

answers to question 6 in the individual study questions. Is there any way that we as women in the new millennium could be involved in telling this story "in memory of her"?

5. The change in the church after Pentecost was quite remarkable, and the experience of God's Spirit was tangible and daily.

> a. If you feel comfortable doing so, share an experience you've had of God's presence (see question 7 in the individual study questions).

> b. Consider together Maria's experience of the Spirit (in chapter 3) and your experiences. Should they be similar, or is this now and that was then?

> c. How could you be more open to the Spirit of God in your life?

Chapter 4: Mary, Mother of Jesus

Individual Study Questions

Read some of the biblical passages that include references to Mary (Luke 1:26-56; 2:1-52; 8:19-21; 11:27-28; John 2:1-12; 19:25-27; Acts 1:14). Then consider these questions, drawing from your own life experience, the passages, the background, and Mary's story in chapter 4. You may find it helpful to write down some of your responses in a journal.

1. How have you "bought" the image of the mother of Jesus as history and myth have presented it? How has that affected your sense of being able to relate to her?

2. As women, we have often been given a sense of the virgin Mary's yes as a sort of passive "whatever," or a humble "anything you say, sir." How might you express her words in Luke 1:38, which give more of a sense of her active collaboration with God?

3. Even Mary needs support at the time of God's challenge and calling her; the angel Gabriel follows his cosmic announcement (Luke

1:35) with a word that sounds like gossip (Luke 1:36), so important is it that she go and get some encouragement. Who is your "Elizabeth," similarly struggling to follow God, who can encourage and speak truth to you?

> a. When have you needed this kind of support, and where did you find it?
>
> b. Where do you need support right now in your life?

4. What stands out to you from Mary's song (Luke 1:46-55)? Try putting the Magnificat into your own words.

5. One of the biggest challenges we face as disciples is that of getting stuck. We may stop sensing God's love for us; we may feel disenfranchised from the Christian community; we may be caught up in many distractions. Or we may get our priorities wrong. And we get stuck, and we stop growing. I believe that one of the places we see this challenge most clearly is in the life of Mary, the mother of Jesus.

> a. Most of us have felt like Mary in terms of being comfortable and then having to push beyond that, as she did at Cana. Where can you relate to this in your life?

6. Mary, more than most of us, must have been tempted to find herself in her role as mother, and yet Jesus didn't allow her to remain in that (Luke 8:19-21; 11:27-28). Are there roles you've been tempted to find yourself in? How can you step out of them?

Group Study Questions

1. As a group, talk about your impressions of Mary, mother of Jesus, from your early religious education, your experience of art, and so on. What has made the strongest impression on you?

2. Can Mary's response in Luke 1 be transformed from the passive victim's "okay" to a collaborative response, or is that wishful thinking? Could she have said no? Share your answers to question 2 in the individual study questions.

3. Many of us were raised in homes in which we were taught to be independent and not to need other people. Luke's account of Mary being sent to Elizabeth underlines the necessity of support, especially when we're hatching some new, risky plan.

a. Share with the group a time when you've been in a situation where you've needed support and someone has been there.

b. Share a place in your life where you are finding that kind of support now. Who is your "Elizabeth"? What are you hatching?

4. Share your answers to question 6 in the individual study questions. What roles have you been tempted to play and to find yourself stuck in?

a. Motherhood is a wonderful thing, but often it has been made into the "be all and end all," which is what this woman was saying when Jesus said "no" (Luke 11:27-28). Jesus has been accused of being antifamily, based on these and some other verses in the Gospels. (See, for instance, Matthew 10:37-38 and 12:46-49; Mark 3:31-35; Luke 8:19-21 and 14:26.) How do we understand Jesus' radical stance here? How is it applied today? How should it be?

5. Mary, the mother of Jesus, stands on a pedestal, quite unapproachable. How can we as women get her back as a model? What can we do to reclaim this character?

Chapter 5: Joanna

Individual Study Questions

There is very little mention of Joanna in the New Testament; along with others, she is referred to in Luke 8:1-3 and 24:1-12. Read those passages, and then consider these questions, drawing from your own life experience, the passages, the background, and Joanna's story in chapter 5. You may find it helpful to write down some of your responses in a journal.

1. In her decision to follow Jesus, Joanna made some tough choices. If she had come to you while she was making that decision, how would you have counseled her? How would you have made a similar decision in her circumstances?

2. Martin Luther's great hymn includes these very challenging words: "Let goods and kindred go, / This mortal life also; / The body they may kill; / God's truth abideth still, / His kingdom is forever." This all sounds a bit fanatical. In your opinion, is it? Have you ever felt that you were being called to make anything like the choices that Joanna or the rich young man make? If you were to set down some principles to use in making that sort of decision, what would they be?

3. Joanna had to make decisions about where she belonged in relation to tradition and in relation to her convictions about the way the new Christian movement ought to be. This is a dilemma most of us who are involved in the church or in any other Christian institution face.

> a. How do you make decisions about where and when to compromise, allowing for differences of conscience, and where and when to stand up for what you believe is right and God's ideal?
>
> b. How much of the way we make these decisions is based on personality type, and how much on Christian maturity or some other factor? Does our way of making these decisions change over our lifetimes?
>
> c. Think of a specific situation in which you've had to make this kind of decision and how you made it. What principles does Joanna use? What principles do you use in deciding what to keep and what to throw out?

4. What does a character like Joanna say to you about your life and choices?

Group Study Questions

1. In your group, share your responses to question 1 in the individual study questions. How would you have counseled Joanna if, say, she had arrived at your group meeting tonight and was trying to decide whether to leave the palace and her husband to follow Jesus?

2. Share your responses to question 2 in the individual study questions: for example, whether you have felt that you've been asked to make a tough choice like Joanna or the rich young man.

3. Referring to Martin Luther's hymn, how does the church today relate to these words? Does it sing them but not act on them; does it say yes, this is where we stand; does it hope this was for a particular time and place? How *should* the church relate to these words? Do you think that some people have to make radical decisions under certain circumstances, or are radical decisions required of all of us?

4. Discuss together your ideas about compromise, freedom, and idealism. Several people should share a time when they've had to make a decision like Joanna's. Then, together, figure out what principles guided Joanna in making her decision, and what principles guided (and should guide) a person today in making that kind of decision.

5. As a group, decide what are the most important things Joanna has to say to contemporary women.

Chapter 6: The Samaritan Woman

Individual Study Questions

Read through chapter 4 of John slowly. Then consider these questions, drawing from your own life experiences, the scriptural passage, the background, and Suheir's story found in chapter 6. You may find it helpful to write down some of your responses in a journal.

1. What are some of the things that might have made this woman feel unworthy or bad? After you list them, try to categorize them.

For instance, if she feels bad about being a Samaritan, you might want to say that this is an area where she is feeling bad about something over which she has no control.

2. If you met Jesus at the well, what would make you feel unworthy or bad, as if Jesus wouldn't really care for you? (If you need help getting started, think of some of your categories above, areas where Suheir felt unloved. Where have you felt those in your own life?)

3. Thirst is not a bad thing. Jesus wouldn't have been sitting near the well had he not been thirsty; the woman wouldn't have been there, either. Focus on thirst:

> a. What would an outsider looking at this woman have assumed she was thirsty for? What was her real thirst?

> b. What would an outsider looking at your life assume you are thirsty for? (Hints: what appears to be most important to you? On what do you spend most of your time, energy, money, and talents?) Jesus sees beyond your apparent thirst to your deep inner thirst. What are you truly, deeply thirsty for?

4. Jesus chose this metaphor of water carefully. In a dry country, water was very important. And water was part of a woman's responsibility; she had to get water for her family to survive. Jesus takes something so vital and ordinary and gives it a whole new meaning. Look at how Jesus talks about water in this passage—as living, gushing out, and so on.

> a. You have identified the thirst in your life. What stops you from drinking deeply of the living water? (There may be many answers here, ranging from small things like ringing phones to big ones like fear or a destructive image of God.)

> b. Spend a few minutes imagining a spring of water deep within your soul. Now imagine the water cleansing you, refreshing you, and making you whole. Draw a picture or write in your journal about how this makes you feel. Can you ask God to deeply satisfy your thirst?

5. The woman at the well drops her water jar and heads off to tell her friends. She has been an outcast, but now she has an important story to tell and a sense of others who need to hear it.

    a. In a sentence or two, summarize her message to you.

    b. What's the story you have to tell, the living water you have to share? With whom has God asked you to share your message?

Group Study Questions

Read John 4 aloud.

1. As you settle in for your discussion, have each person share a time when water was meaningful or significant to them.

2. Share from your answers to question 1 in the individual study questions, listing some of the things that might have made this woman feel unworthy or bad. Are there things on Suheir's "unworthy" list that you can relate to or find parallels with in your lives? Should some of these things have made this woman feel unworthy? Are some of the things that you've shared from your own lives legitimate reasons to feel unworthy or rejected?

3. Go around and have everyone in the group share their answer to question 3a in the individual study questions: what was Suheir's real thirst? Discuss together your sense of how her real thirst relates to her faith. Do you sense that this woman expected her faith to meet her thirst, does she vaguely hope it will, or does she not expect any real answers from her faith?

4. How does your thirst relate to your faith? Are you like Suheir in your expectations of how your deep thirst will be met by your faith?

5. Share with the group what you feel your real thirst is and what stops you from drinking deeply to satisfy it. Pray for each other, that like this woman we may all bring our thirst to God and be deeply satisfied.

6. In closing, share your answers to 5a in the individual study questions: "Suheir's message to me is . . ." Then, as a group, write one or two sentences that answer this question: What is Suheir's message to women today? Have someone write down what you come up with.

Chapter 7: Martha

Individual Study Questions

Read some of the biblical passages that include references to Martha (Luke 10:48-52; John 11:1-53; 12:1-2). Then consider these questions, drawing from your own life experience, the passages, the background, and Martha's story in chapter 7. You will find it helpful to write down some of your responses in a journal.

1. The passage in Luke 10 is remarkable partly because it seems so ordinary, so everyday, and yet it is in those ordinary moments that we find the great patterns of our lives. Look at Martha here:

   a. When have you felt the kind of frustration that she is feeling?

   b. Why do you think she decides to go to Jesus with her problem?

2. Martha comes to Jesus and essentially says, "Lord, I can't do it all . . . ." What do you bring with you when you come to Jesus, saying, "Lord, I can't do it all . . ."?

   a. Jesus tells Martha that she is "worried and distracted by many things." If Jesus was speaking to you, what would he say? "[Your Name], you are worried and distracted by. . . ." List what you are worried and distracted by.

   b. Jesus seems to be saying to Martha that compared to her sister, she has been trivialized by others, or she has trivialized herself. Do you ever feel that your time is trivialized, that others don't value what you do adequately, that you, perhaps, don't value your time enough?

c. Jesus says to Martha: "Only one thing is necessary . . ."
What is Jesus calling you to say yes to? Think about your
"one necessary thing" and saying yes to the call of Christ.

3. When we see Martha later in the book of John she speaks some
of the great words of faith. Look at these verses (John 11:20-27).
What do Martha's words seem to say about her growing faith?

4. In John 12, we see Martha serving, which many scholars agree
speaks to her probable role in the early church as one who presided
at the eucharistic meal. This makes a fascinating overlap, the centrality of the table and of hospitality, but taken deeper and given the
blessing of the church.

a. What gifts do you have that may have grown in this way,
from early interests and inclinations to more fully developed ministries?

b. As you consider your "one necessary thing," consider
what might come out of your early inclinations and bear
mature fruit in your life now, as it did in Martha's.

Group Discussion Questions

1. As a group, list some of the ideals you've felt pressured to be, for
example, "a good woman" or " a good Christian." One way to get at
this is to think about the messages that you were given as you were
growing up (in school, in church, at home): to dress, act, speak, or
keep your room in a certain way. Complete these sentences: "Good
girls always . . ." and "Good girls never . . ." (As a group, you should
have no problem coming up with thirty or forty.)

a. Do you think your mother felt the same pressures you
did? Do your daughters (or other younger people)?

b. Which of these pressures still feel oppressive to you? As
a group, decide on three or four.

2. Martha felt tremendous pressure to perform. She seems to have
been very busy, but at some level frustrated, bored, and trivialized.

Share your answers to questions 1a, 2a, and 2b in the individual study questions, focusing on your feelings that parallel Martha's.

3. When I point out to groups that the great words of faith we hear from Peter in the other Gospels, which are supposed to have made him the rock on which the church is built and the first pope, are the words of Martha in the Gospel of John, they often react with disbelief. If we believe that Martha said these words as well as Peter, does it make a difference to our understanding of women and the faith?

4. Discuss together the continuity between Martha's early obsession with the table and hospitality and her later calling to preside at the table. Does this mean that her gifts are all natural talents, that God uses natural talents, or that God had given her those original gifts and interests to bear mature fruit later? How do you understand the relationship between early interests and talents and a person's calling in the church?

> a. Share with the group what you think might be the "one thing" that Jesus says is necessary to you. Or to get at it another way, share from your answer to question 4 in the individual study questions: what early talent or interest of yours might begin to bear mature fruit?
>
> b. Leave time to pray together about what you need to say no and yes to in your lives.

Chapter 8: The Meeting

Individual Study Questions

1. The word *eucharist* means "to give thanks." The gathered women here are giving thanks for calling, belonging, understanding, love, and more. What work of God in your life would you like to give thanks for?

2. Often God most clearly speaks to us through our sisters and brothers. How has this been true for you?

3. Which of the women in *Spirited Women* have you been able to most fully relate to; which has spoken to you most clearly? Reread your notes about your work with her, and then write a letter to yourself from her. Include in this letter all that you think she would like to tell you: about things in you that might make her happy, her concerns for you, and her words of encouragement and challenge. Let her speak to you for a page or two.

Group Discussion Questions

1. Remembering that the word *eucharist* means "to give thanks," begin by going around the circle and letting each person say something for which they are thankful during the time this group has been together. (You may want to draw from questions 1 and 2 in the individual study questions.)

2. Go around the circle and have each person read the letter they have from their foremother. Pray for each other in one or all of the following ways: Use whatever method of prayer you feel most comfortable with.

> a. Like the women in *Spirited Women*, gather around each woman and pray for her after she has shared her letter. This is an opportunity to pray about some of the issues she has raised in the letter. (For this kind of prayer, it is often helpful to have a footstool in the center of the circle that each person takes a turn sitting on.)
>
> b. Follow each person's sharing time with a time of silent prayer for the woman who has shared.
>
> c. Join hands at the end of the session and have each person, silently or aloud, pray for the woman on her right.

3. End by saying aloud together some of the prayers within this last chapter, ending with the blessing.

Notes
for Further Reading

❧

Prologue

Women's presence in the early church: These earliest years are often
called the "primitive church." For an overview of this period, see
W. H. C. Frend, *The Rise of Christianity* (Philadelphia: Fortress
Press, 1984). The complexity of finding the women in this period is
partly based on the sources available.

We can see the women in the scriptures themselves, but this
often involves reading between the lines. All the Gospels refer to a
group of women who were present at the crucifixion; see Matthew
27:55-56; Mark 40:14-41; Luke 23:49; John 19:25. We can see a number of women active in ministry in the earliest church, for instance,
those mentioned in Acts 12:12; Romans 16; 1 Corinthians 11:5;
Colossians 4:15; and 2 Timothy 1:5 and 4:19. See also Acts 21:9,
where Phillip had a number of daughters who prophesied. Priscilla
taught Apollos (Acts 18:24-28). Referring to Romans 16:7, even St.
John Chrysostom wrote this of Junia: "Oh how great is the devotion
of this woman that she should be counted worthy of the appellation
of apostle!" See *The Homilies of St. John Chrysostom: Nicene and
Post-Nicene Fathers* (Grand Rapids, Mich.: Eerdmans, 1956).

For other sources on the New Testament and women in this
very early period, I suggest Martin Hengel's *Acts and the History of
Earliest Christianity*, trans. John Bowden (Philadelphia: Fortress

Press, 1979) and his book *Between Jesus and Paul: Studies in the Earliest History of Christianity*, trans. John Bowden (Philadelphia: Fortress Press, 1983). See also Ross Shepard Kraemer's *Her Share of the Blessings: Women's Religions among Pagans, Jews, and Christians in the Greco-Roman World* (New York: Oxford University Press, 1992), 156; Elisabeth Schüssler Fiorenza's *In Memory of Her: A Feminist Theological Reconstruction of Christian Origins* (New York: Crossroad, 1994), 177–80, 217; Frend's *Rise of Christianity*, especially 55; Roger Gryson's *The Ministry of Women in the Early Church*, trans. Jean Laporte and Mary Louise Hall (Collegeville, Minn.: Liturgical Press, 1976), 2; Susanne Heine's *Women and Early Christianity: A Reappraisal*, trans. John Bowden (Minneapolis: Augsburg Publishing House, 1988), 20; and Elizabeth Moltmann-Wendel's *The Women around Jesus*, trans. John Bowden (New York: Crossroad, 1982), 131–44.

The New Testament picture of the women followers is complex. For instance, Luke often refers to the women in terms of their wealth and prominence—see Acts 17:4-12—but forgets to point out their importance to the movement as a whole. See Fiorenza, *In Memory of Her*, 90, 177.

We also see shifts in the New Testament itself. Early in the second century, one generation after Paul, there are intimations of change in the Pastoral Epistles, and it has been suggested that the church responded to persecution by conforming more with society in general and by forming more ecclesiastical organizations. See James D. G. Dunn, *Unity and Diversity in the New Testament* (Philadelphia: Westminster, 1977), 114. On the other hand, in John 12:12, Martha is referred to in a way that would, by the time it was written, imply an official ministry in the church. Raymond Brown, in his "Roles of Women in the Fourth Gospel" (*Theological Studies* 36, 1975), 690, writes: "We are told that Martha served at table *(diakonein)*. On the story level of Jesus' ministry this might not seem significant; but the evangelist is writing in the 90s C.E., when the office of *diakonos* already existed in the post-Pauline churches (see the Pastorals) and when the task of waiting on tables was a specific function to which the community or its leaders appointed individuals by the laying on of hands (Acts 6:1-6)."

Another way of judging women's place in earliest Christianity is by comparing it with their role in wider society. For instance, compare the women's actions in Acts to what the Talmud says of the purpose of marriage, in which a woman is to "grind corn, suckle children, be a beautiful wife, and bear children." See Hengel, *Acts,*120, and Mary Evans, *Woman in the Bible* (London: InterVarsity Press, 1978), 49–51. It seems that within either Jewish or Greco-Roman society, family was an oppressive unit to women. For the Roman woman, the idea of paterfamilias dominated; the antifamily ethos of early Christianity moved women outside these pressures; early metaphors for the Christian church were Jesus and the body of Christ, not family. See Fiorenza, *In Memory of Her,* 183.

We can also find information on women in contemporary sources, some sympathetic and some critical. For instance, stories of early women martyrs are preserved in *Passion of Perpetua and Felicitas,* who died in 203 c.e. in Carthage, North Africa. For more information, see Peter Dronke, *Women Writers of the Middle Ages: A Critical Study of Texts from Perpetua to Marguerite Porete* (Cambridge, N.Y.: Cambridge University Press, 1984), 60–82.

Some contemporary writers were critical of Christianity partly because of its attitude toward women, such as Celsus, who wrote about the church in the second century. For more on this, see Margaret Y. MacDonald, *Early Christian Woman and Pagan Opinion* (Cambridge, N.Y.: Cambridge University Press, 1996), 82–94. It seems that men's role in society often went down on their joining the movement, while women's went up. See Kraemer, *Her Share of the Blessings,*144–56; and Fiorenza, *In Memory of Her,* 180.

Because of the variety and "patchiness" of these sources, the imagination becomes a helpful tool. In my book *The Magdalene Gospel* (New York: Doubleday, 1995), I try to reconstruct the women's place during the ministry of Jesus, the crucifixion, and Holy Saturday. For more on imaginative reconstruction, see Nicholas Wolterstorff's in *Divine Discourse: Philosophical Reflections on the Claim that God Speaks* (New York: Cambridge University Press, 1995), chap. 14. Fiorenza invokes the historic imagination: "Women's actual contribution to the early Christian missionary movement largely remains lost because of the scarcity and androcentric character of our sources. It must be rescued through historical imagination as well as in and through reconstruction of this movement that fills out and contextualizes the fragmentary information still available to us . . . they are the tip of the iceberg" (*In Memory of Her*, 168).

Midrash: For more on midrash, see Gary C. Porton, "Defining Midrash," in *The Study of Ancient Judaism,* ed. Jacob Neusner (New York: KTAV, 1981); Nahum Glatzer, *Hammer on the Rock: A Midrash Reader* (New York: Schocken Books, 1962); and Jacob Neusner, *What is Midrash?* (Philadelphia: Fortress Press, 1987), 13, 103.

Chapter 1: Lost and Found at the Table

Worship in the earliest church: In the primitive church, house churches were a new way of worshiping; they generally met in the larger homes of well-to-do Christians. The first day of the week had tremendous significance because of the resurrection. Included in the house church would have been the whole family, servants, and other Christians who lived close by. In Jerusalem, house meetings were added to temple worship: by Acts 2:42, 46, this was already happening.

By Acts 2:42, you have this balance of ritual reenactment of and sharing in the Lord's supper. There was a powerful eschatological emphasis in the eucharist. The women would wonder what it would be like to celebrate the eucharist away from Jerusalem. See Frederick J. Cwiekowski, *The Beginnings of the Church* (New York: Paulist Press, 1988) 76–77. Certain other liturgical practices are in evidence early on, such as the "holy kiss" and the idea of "anathema," although there seems to have been tremendous diversity in worship in the early church. See Hengel, *Between Jesus and Paul*, 81, and Dunn, *Unity and Diversity,* 120, 132–39. Other parts of worship may have included the reading of a text and its explication and application by a speaker. See 1 Corinthians 14 for a sense of the group interaction in these early meetings. For more on this, see Cwiekowski, *Beginnings of the Church*, 118–19; Hans Conzelman, *History of Primitive Christianity*, trans. John E. Steely (Nashville: Abingdon, 1973), 128; and Fiorenza, *In Memory of Her*, 177.

In Palestinian Jewish Christianity, songs such as those in Luke 1 and 2 were used, as well as psalms and doxologies. See Cwiekowski, *Beginnings of the Church*, 77, and Luke 2:29-32; 1:39-53. See also S. Farris, "Hymns in Luke's Infancy Narrative," *Journal for the Study of the New Testament* 9 (October 1985).

In Hellenistic churches, the praise seems to have been more exuberant, and there were also songs that turn up in the letters and Gospels. See Philippians 2:6-11; Colossians 1:15-20; John 1: 1-16; Acts 15:28.

Stephen, James, and groups in the earliest church: For more on Stephen and some of the conflicts in the earliest church, see chapter 5: Joanna. Stephen's story is told in Acts 6 and 7, where he can be seen to be strongly associated with wisdom, grace, and the power of the Spirit. Another key player in these early days was James, the brother of Jesus, who was converted after the resurrection. For more on James, see Acts 1:13; 12:7, 15; 21:18; Galatians 2:9, 12. Some of the Aramaic-speaking Christians like James might have felt that Stephen was being a bit extreme and outspoken. These Christians went daily to the temple, as can be seen in Acts 2:46; 3:1; 5:12, 25, 42. Some scholars argue that Peter lost some of his authority in Jerusalem through being on the fence on these issues. See Dunn, *Unity and Diversity,* 245.

Also present were the radical itinerant communities who took seriously Jesus' words on having nowhere to lay one's head and giving away all of one's possessions. For more on these groups, see

Gerd Theissen, *Social Reality and the Early Christians: Theology, Ethics, and the World of the New Testament,* trans. Margaret Kohl, (Minneapolis: Fortress Press, 1992*); The Social Setting of Pauline Christianity: Essays on Corinth,* ed. and trans., and with an introduction by John H. Schütz, (Philadelphia: Fortress Press, 1982); and *Sociology of Early Palestinian Christianity,* trans. John Bowden (Philadelphia: Fortress Press, 1978).

In the early church, one of the questions followers had to work out was how radical to be: would you be more or less radical than Jesus? The women had met and followed Jesus, and left families and possessions; many had renounced a fixed abode. It seems that the Palestinian church emphasized homelessness, lack of possessions, and lack of family, while other parts of the church felt the need to adjust to society (since Jesus wasn't coming back immediately). Galilee was the center for the male and female missionaries, the itinerant preachers; believers there set the standard for other on-the-road missionaries. See Pheme Perkins, *Ministering in the Pauline Churches* (New York: Paulist Press, 1982), 14–20. It seems likely to me that some of the women returned to Galilee and joined the more radical itinerant group there.

Luke: According to Hengel, Luke was a writer who delighted in shaping his materials. He wrote Acts from two main sources—a collection of the accounts of Peter and an Antiochene source who emerges in chapter 6. Hengel writes that Luke had one clear idea in writing, "to describe the ideal world mission, that is the mission of Paul. His work is a deliberate history of the Pauline mission with an extended introduction." See *Between Jesus and Paul,* 4–10, 55. Some scholars conclude that one of Luke's sources must have been a woman, because he includes so many stories about them. Others have argued that she might have been a widow. For more on this, see Leonard Swidler's *Biblical Affirmations for Women* (Philadelphia: Westminster, 1977), 259–60.

Phillip: For more on Phillip, see John 21:17; Acts 6:1-7, 8:4-40. Notice that Phillip even spoke to an Ethiopian eunuch—one who could never be part of the faith, and who was from what seemed like the ends of the earth. For more about Jewish relationships with those outside the faith, see Frend, *Rise of Christianity*, 18, and Hengel, *Acts*, 79–80. For more on the Samaritan woman, see chapter 6, and John 4.

Words of Jesus: Jesus' words and the stories of his actions were treasured by the early church, and eyewitnesses were highly valued. Often few written records were made because of the expectation of Jesus' quick return. Some of the most treasured stories about Jesus were the passion accounts, the sayings of Jesus, and the miracle accounts—these formed the heart of the believers' teachings and practices. For more on this, see Dunn, *Unity and Diversity*, 75, 128.

Chapter 2: Mary Magdalene

Mary Magdalene: Mary Magdalene was known as the "apostle to the apostles," because she met the risen Jesus first and was given the message to take to the hiding male disciples. See Matthew 28:10; Mark 16:11-13; Luke 24:8-12; John 20:17-18. The "official teaching" of the Jerusalem church that Paul says he "received" (1 Corinthians 15:3-8) does not include Mary Magdalene, probably because, as a woman, she was not considered an appropriate witness in a Jewish context.

For more on Mary Magdalene, see my book *The Magdalene Gospel*. Also in the whole of her book, *Mary Magdalene: Myth and Metaphor* (New York: Harcourt, Brace and Co., 1993), Susan Haskins looks at shifts in understandings of Mary Magdalene, tracing them in art and literature. See also Raymond Brown's "Roles of Women in the Fourth Gospel," 692–94; Kevin Coyle, "The Fathers On Women," in *Women in Early Christianity;* David M. Scholer, ed., *Women in Early Christianity,* Studies in Early Christianity, vol. 14 (New York: Garland, 1993), 120; Marina Warner, in her book on Mary, mother of Jesus, has a chapter on Mary Magdalene (see *Alone of All Her Sex: The Myth and the Cult of the Virgin Mary* [New York: Vintage, 1983]).

Marys: For more on the confusion of Marys, see John 12:1-3; Mark 14:3; and Matthew 26:6-7. The confusion of Mary Magdalene with Mary of Bethany, and with the "sinful woman" who anoints Jesus, goes back to the second century. For Mary Magdalene to be relegated to the role of ever repenting sinner, rather than "apostle to the apostles," she had to be associated with sexual sin. Catholic scholars now see this confusion of Marys as a willful disregard of scripture to underline the church's ascetic program. For a history of this mistake, see Haskins, *Mary Magdalene*, 16–31, and chapter 5. See also chapters 4 and 5 of Warner's *Alone of All Her Sex.*

Chapter 3: Maria, Sister of Martha

Maria: Like Mary Magdalene, Mary, sister of Martha, has been a victim of name confusion, which is why I call her Maria. To read the scriptural accounts about her, see Luke 10:39-42; John 11:1-44. For her role in anointing Jesus, see John 12:1-8; Matthew 26:6-13, and *The Magdalene Gospel.* See also Haskins, *Mary Magdalene*, 7, 16–26, 58–60, 62–63, 90–9; and Gryson, *The Ministry of Women in the Early Church*, 2.

To contrast Jesus' call to Maria to sit and listen to him teach with the cultural norms of his time, see Frend, *Rise of Christianity*, 67. Women, according to Frend, couldn't teach or bear witness. "Better burn the Torah than teach it to a woman" was a saying of the rabbi Eliezer in c. 90, for "she was in all things inferior to a man." See also Evans, *Woman in the Bible*, 47–53.

Women disciples: Consider the social pressures against Jesus' calling women to follow him. Respectable women in first-century Judaism and society should not be seen in public; they couldn't speak to a man in public; they could not be taught the Torah; they could never follow a rabbi; they could not make ethical decisions without the supervision of a father or husband. See Evans, *Women in the Bible.*, 44–57. Women had access to God only through the patriarchal family: "Women are sanctified through the deeds of men." See Jacob Neusner, *Method and Meaning in Ancient Judaism*,

Brown Judaic Studies: Third Series (Missoula, Mont.: Scholars Press, 1979), 100.

Church historian Frend says this of Jesus' attitude toward women: "Indeed, his attitude towards women was revolutionary, and may have contributed to his final break with the Pharisees" (*The Rise of Christianity*, 67). Jesus' break here was so radically countercultural that we have still not caught up with him nearly twenty centuries later. For more on this, see my book *Balancing Act: How Women Can Lose Their Roles and Find Their Callings* (Downers Grove, Ill.: InterVarsity Press, 1996), 67–75; and Dorothy L. Sayers, "The-Human-Not-Quite-Human," in *Are Women Human?* (Grand Rapids, Mich.: Eerdmans, 1971), 46.

Crucifixion: All the Gospels refer to a group of women who were present at the crucifixion. See Matthew 27:55-56; Mark 40:14-41; Luke 23:49; and John 19:25. In Judaism, the nakedness of the crucifixion was shame indeed, and the shame was often on the ones who witnessed the nakedness. See Genesis 9:18-27, Leviticus 23:16; Deuteronomy 16:12, 16; 21:23; Mark 14:50; and Philippians 2:8. For a discussion of crucifixion in this time, see Martin Hengel, *Crucifixion in the Ancient World and the Folly of the Message of the Cross,* trans. John Bowden (Philadelphia: Fortress Press, 1977), particularly 87–88.

It was known that to be at the crucifixion or the tomb of a crucified criminal was dangerous, and yet the women were there. See my book *The Magdalene Gospel*, and also Luise Schottroff's "Maria Magdalena und die Frauen am Grabe," trans. Kirk Allison (Evangelische Theologie 42, 1982), 3–35, especially 6ff.

Pentecost: For scriptural references to Pentecost, see Acts 1 and 2; Luke 24:44-49; and John 20:21-23.

Chapter 4: Mary, Mother of Jesus

Mary: The mother of Jesus figures in a number of biblical texts, including Matthew 1:18-25; 12:46-50; Luke 1:26—2:52; 11:27;

Acts 1:14. See also my book *The Magdalene Gospel*, 90–94; and Brown, "Roles of Women in the Fourth Gospel," 695–97.

The most comprehensive book on the way the virgin Mary has been used throughout history is Marina Warner's *Alone of All Her Sex*. She summarizes, for instance, the very popular apocryphal book The *Gospel of James*, which is the great source for information on Mary's childhood, Saint Anne's childhood, and so forth. *The Book of James* goes on to Jesus' childhood in Nazareth, telling how occasionally, when a playmate irritated him by knocking down his mud play, Jesus would strike him dead. Warner also points out that there was a period in which it was acceptable to portray Mary suckling Jesus, and even to meditate on being suckled at her breasts; her milk became a big mover in the relic trade. See Warner, *Alone of All Her Sex*, chapter 13. Mary also became associated with courtly love. See C. S. Lewis, *The Allegory of Love: A Study in Medieval Tradition* (Oxford: Clarendon Press, 1936), 11; Warner, *Alone of All Her Sex*, chapter 11; and Dante's *Divine Comedy*. Warner also traces the doctrine of Mary's bodily assumption. Although some said she died of sorrow as she lived and relived the death of her son, and others that she faked a death out of humility, her bodily assumption means Mary is set apart from the human race, not touched by the fall. Warner shows how Mary ultimately came to be crowned queen of heaven and associated with the church triumphant in Revelations 21:2; 22:17. Ultimately Mary herself, even if she is not holding Jesus, is worthy of some kind of worship. See Warner, *Alone of All Her Sex*, 251.

Virginity: Attitudes toward virginity shift dramatically during the first five hundred years of the church. If we consider the Jewish context, virginity was good, but marriage and a quiver full of children was better. Sara and Hannah bemoan their lack of fertility: childlessness is seen as a curse. Despite the positive value society placed on fertility and childbirth, these very qualities made women subject to ritual impurity. For material on women's impurity, see Leviticus 12:2-5; 15:23-24; Swidler, *Biblical Affirmations for Women*, 46–149; Kraemer, *Her Share of the Blessings*, 99–102; and Evans, *Women in the Bible*, 24–26.

Greco-Roman thinking was more consistently antiflesh. The idea of incarnation was also repugnant to Roman understanding; the gods wouldn't do something like that, because the body is a hindrance to escape. See Everett Ferguson, *Backgrounds of Early Christianity* (Grand Rapids, Mich.: Eerdmans, 1993), 572. Augustine had been deeply affected by the teachings of Mani and the influences of Gnosticism, which added to Platonic disdain for flesh (see Warner, *Alone of All Her Sex*, 54). After the conversion of Constantine and the Edict of Milan, Christians were no longer attacked from without. Some argue that they felt they needed to bring hardships on themselves, and this they did by increasing their asceticism. In this new way of thinking, virginity came to be associated with spiritual power. Virginity was the wholeness created by God; marriage was buying into a fallen state. Virginity reduced some of the penalties of the fall that could be seen in women (see Warner, *Alone of all Her Sex*, 70). To see how the church has valued its women saints as virgins, see listings of saints' days or *Foxe's Book of Martyrs* (John Foxe, various editions [1856]).

Magnificat: Mary's song, found in Luke 1:39-53, finds its source in 1 Samuel 2:1-11. It's wonderful for us as women to ponder how the Magnificat became one of the hymns of the early church. The preacher was pregnant that day, bearing the holy one. The church, of course, has used the Magnificat as sung by boy sopranos, because women were not allowed near the altar (in case they were menstruating or pregnant). The version of the Magnificat used in *Spirited Women* was written by Janet Morley and appears in *All Desires Known*, (London: SPCK, 1998), 76.

Chapter 5: Joanna

Joanna: Not much is known about Joanna: biblical references are limited to Luke 8:1-3; 24:9; and, perhaps, Matthew 27:55; Mark 15:40; and Luke 23:49. Herod's court is mentioned in Matthew 14:1-12.

Aramaic Jewish Christians: For more information on the Aramaic Jewish Christians, see James D. G. Dunn, *Parting of the Ways* (London: SCM, 1991); and Ian Hazlett, ed., *Early Christianity: Origins and Evolution to* A.D. *600* (Nashville: Abingdon, 1991). Christianity was not the first Messianic sect within Judaism, but it was rare in that it was centered in Jerusalem and not the countryside. See Frend, *Rise of Christianity,* 25; Abraham Malherbe, *Social Aspects of Early Christianity* (Baton Rouge: Louisiana State University Press, 1977), 30; Hans Joachim Kraus, *Worship in Israel: A Cultic History of the Old Testament,* trans. Geoffrey Buswell (Richmond: John Knox, 1966), 253–58; and Conzelman, *History of Primitive Christianity,* 44.

Aramaic Jewish Christians worshiped in the temple, which is evident in Acts 2:46; 3:1; 5:20, 42, as well as in Hengel, *Between Jesus and Paul,* 58–59. It is not clear whether the Hellenist believers continued to go to the temple, or perhaps went to the temple less frequently than their Aramaic counterparts. See Cwiekowski, *Beginnings of the Church,* 73–82. The Aramaic Christians believed circumcision was important. See Genesis 17:10-11; Acts 15:5; 21:20. It seems that the Jerusalem church took the synagogue model for their governance, with a body of elders. It was more rigid, less charismatic and spontaneous. Perhaps this is why the model of the Twelve worked so well in Jerusalem. See Dunn, *Unity and Diversity,* 109.

Much of the New Testament is the story of the church coming to terms with the question Dunn expresses this way: "How can Gentiles be included within the Messianic community of Israel?" *Jesus, Paul, and the Law: Studies in Mark and Galatians* (Louisville, Ky.: Westminster John Knox, 1990), 131.

Hellenistic Jewish Christians: "By the time of Christ, Judaism was the single most vital religious movement in the Greco-Roman world," writes church historian Frend in *The Rise of Christianity,* 42. This is why at that first Pentecost, Peter is able to preach to Jews after they have responded to hearing their own languages spoken. See Acts 2:5-6. In *The Beginnings of the Church,* 99, Cwiekowski points out that Priscilla and Aquila must have already been Christians by the 40s, presumably from that preaching in Acts. For more on these Hellenistic Jewish believers, see Frend, *Rise of Christianity,* 18–20, 40; Hazlett, *Early Christianity,* 42, 65; and Fiorenza, *In Memory of Her,* 162–68.

Paul was a Hellenistic Jew who became a Christian. He was from Tarsus, a bustling Greek city. For biblical references, see Acts 9:2; 19:9. For more on Paul's attitudes, see Cwiekowski, *Beginnings of the Church,* 77, 88; Dunn, *Unity and Diversity,* 109; Dunn, *Parting of the Ways,* 221–22; and Fiorenza, *In Memory of Her,* 54, 66–67, 73–76, 110. It is remarkable how quickly Paul came to understand who Jesus was, and how well developed his Christology was, even early on. See Dunn, *Unity and Diversity,* 224–240, and Hengel, *Between Jesus and Paul,* 40–41.

Widows: Widows were seen as reproached by God, forsaken, helpless, and exposed to harsh treatment. See Bonnie Bowman Thurston, *The Widows: A Women's Ministry in the Early Church* (Philadelphia: Fortress Press, 1989). See also Hengel, *Between Jesus and Paul,* 15, and Joseph B. Tyson, *The New Testament and Early Christianity* (New York: Macmillan, 1984), 287–93.

The split: Hellenistic Jews were the ones who attacked Stephen. See Acts 6:1-14. Luke is careful in selecting materials, and yet he quotes Stephen's sermon extensively in Acts 7:2-53. His sermon is inflammatory to his listeners: Stephen uses words associated with the Holy Spirit, and many references to Moses, who was associated with special wisdom and the Spirit. For more on this split, see Frend, *Rise of Christianity,* 26; Hengel, *Acts,* 74; Hengel, *Between Jesus and Paul,* 18, 24; and Dunn, *Unity and Diversity,* 128.

The spread of the message: By the year 40 c.e., there were many more Christians who had never met Jesus than those who had. In *Between Jesus and Paul,* Hengel writes that this time, when a message could be taken to all the known world, was short-lived (28–29). For an idea of how much people traveled, note that Priscilla and Aquila are at various times in Pontus, Rome, Corinth, Ephesus, and then back in Rome. Christians seemed to travel a lot, avoiding the inns and staying with other Christians as they traveled: the significance of table fellowship and cross-cultural openness becomes clear. See Malherbe, *Social Aspects of Early Christianity*, 62–66. See also F. F. Bruce, *Paul and Jesus* (Grand Rapids, Mich.: Baker Book House, 1974), 34–35, and Kraemer, *Her Share of the Blessings*, 142–43.

Christianity became the answer to people hungering for a message like Judaism without Judaism's exclusivity, and the Greek language provided the vehicle. See Hengel, *Between Jesus and Paul*, 28–29. Antioch was the center of the movement. See Frend, *Rise of Christianity*, 24, 33, 70–71, 89. Jesus anticipated this openness to those outside the faith, as we can see in Luke 4:25-27 and Matthew 28:16-20. For more on this, see particularly N. T. Wright's *Jesus and the Victory of God*, Christian Origins and the Question of God, vol. 2 (Minneapolis: Fortress Press, 1996). The church figures this out: see Acts 8:2-40. For further reading, see Hengel, *Between Jesus and Paul*, 24–26; *Acts*, 71, 79, 90, and Cwiekowski, *Beginnings of the Church*, 82. See also Everett Ferguson, ed., *Encyclopedia of Early Christianity* (New York: Garland, 1997), 199–201; Fergusen, *Backgrounds of Early Christianity*, 124–25; Thurston, *Widows*, 28–31; and Fiorenza, *In Memory of Her*, 184. Christians eventually came to be seen as a sort of new race between gentiles and Jews. See Hazlett, *Early Christianity*, 66.

Apostles/disciples/the Twelve: Although there is not space here for a full discussion, an apostle in the New Testament seems to have been someone who satisfied the criteria of having seen the risen Jesus and been sent out by him. See Elizabeth M. Tetlow, *Women and Ministry in the New Testament* (New Jersey: Paulist Press, 1980), 116. Also see Dunn, *Unity and Diversity*, 107, where he points out that the grouping "the twelve" is not the same as "the apostles." See 1 Corinthians 15:3-7. For further reading, see K. Giles, *The Patterns of Ministry among the First Christians* (Melbourne: Collins Dove, 1989); and Martin Hengel, *The Charismatic Leader and His Followers*, trans. James Greig (New York: Crossroad, 1981).

Chapter 6: The Samaritan Woman

The Samaritan woman: See John 4:1-42. Scholars see this woman as the first missionary, with a clear missionary function. See Brown, "Roles of Women in the Fourth Gospel," 690–91. Jews were allowed only three marriages, and it is probable that the same standard was applicable to Samaritans, so she would have been seen as markedly immoral. See Brown, *Gospel According to John,* 171. In John 4:27, Brown argues that the phrase for *apostle* is used by Jesus here to refer to the woman who has done the sowing. See Brown, "Roles of Women in the Fourth Gospel," 690.

Samaritan/Jewish relations: The Samaritans refused to worship in Jerusalem. They also made the Jewish restoration of Jerusalem difficult and fought on the side of the Syrian monarchs against the Jews. The Jewish high priest burnt their temple on Mount Gerezim in 128 B.C.E. See Frend, *Rise of Christianity,* 18; Hengel, *Acts,* 78–79; and Swidler, *Biblical Affirmations for Women,* 189. Samaritan expectations of the coming Messiah were not for an anointed king of the house of David, but for a prophet like Moses. See Raymond E. Brown, *The Gospel According to John* (Garden City, N.Y.: Doubleday, 1966), 172.

Evangelism of Samaria: See Acts 8:1-3 for the first missionary movement to Samaria. I'm suggesting for the purposes of this book that Peter and John went to Samaria at the same time Suheir came to Jerusalem (see Acts 8:14-17). Some scholars think it odd that no believers are mentioned when Phillip arrives in Samaria. See Acts 8:4-8 and Hengel, *Acts,* 78–79. Jesus' words to the woman about worshiping in spirit and truth seem much closer to what we see in Stephen's sermon (Acts 7) that led to his being stoned. John seems to be drawing a distinction between the earthbound worship at Jerusalem or Gerezim and the heavenly Spirit-filled worship. This would have been a strong theme for the Hellenistic evangelists who reached Samaria a few years later. See Brown, *Gospel According to John,* 80, and Hengel, *Between Jesus and Paul,* 121–22.

Chapter 7: Martha

To read about Martha in the scriptures, see Luke 10:38-42; John 11; 12:2. Her prominence in the biblical texts leads scholars to believe that she was a leader in the church during the time the Gospels were written. For further reading, see my book *The Magdalene Gospel*; Gryson, *Ministry of Women in the Early Church*, 2; and Brown, "Roles of Women in the Fourth Gospel," 694. Bethany was probably Jesus' "home away from home" in Jerusalem. Because the population of Jerusalem swelled during festivals, many people needed somewhere to stay. See J. Murphy-O'Connor, *The Holy Land: An Archaeological Guide from Earliest Times to 1700*, 3d ed. (New York: Oxford University Press, 1992).

Compare Martha's statement of faith (John 11:27) with Peter's (Matthew 16:16). For more on this, see Brown, "Roles of Women in the Fourth Gospel," 690–91; and Ivoni Richter Reimer, *Women in the Acts of the Apostles: A Feminist Liberation Perspective*, trans. Linda M. Maloney (Minneapolis: Fortress Press, 1995), 236.

Table fellowship: There were 229 laws related to food purity in the Jewish tradition. See Dunn, *Parting of the Ways*, 130–37. To read more about the issue of table purity in the ministry of Jesus, see Mark 7:1-5; Luke 7:36-39; 19:5-7; 22:7-19; 24:13-33; and John 12:3.

As the church grew, this issue became one of the most central, defining who could be a member. See Acts 10:9-16; 11:1-18; 21: 17-26; Galatians 2:11-14. See also Dunn's discussion of table fellowship in *Jesus, Paul, and the Law*, 136–58. For more on this issue, see Frend, *Rise of Christianity*, 67; Cwiekowski, *Beginnings of the Church*, 76–77, 94; Bruce, *Paul and Jesus*, 34–35; and Fiorenza, *In Memory of Her*, 162–68.

In much of classical Greek culture, women didn't dine in public (see Kraemer, *Her Share of the Blessings*, 142). Jewish women, however, were used to being involved in feasts (see Fiorenza, *In Memory of Her*, 87, 176–77). Although there does seem to have been some variation in practice from synagogue to synagogue—see Bernadette J. Brooten, *Women Leaders in the Ancient Synagogue:*

Inscriptional Evidence and Background Issues (Chico, Calif.: Scholars Press, 1982)—the house churches were arguably fellowships of equals. See Fiorenza, *In Memory of Her,* 166.

Growing hostility toward women: As we have seen, there are intimations of change in the Pastoral Epistles. It has been suggested that the church responded to persecutions by conforming more with society in general and by forming more ecclesiastical organizations. See Dunn, *Unity and Diversity,* 114.

The history of the church is one of almost unbroken misogyny. For example, Tertullian wrote scathingly of women who dared to "teach, to participate in theological disputes, to exorcise, to promise healings, and to baptize." Women, he goes on, are not allowed to speak in church, "to fulfill any male function. . . ." Women, he argues, are the "devil's gateway." (See Quintus Terullianus, *Disciplinary, Moral, and Ascetical Works,* trans. Rudolph Arbesmann Sr., et al., (New York: Fathers of the Church, 1959). For more on this topic, see Swidler, *Biblical Affirmations for Women,* 345; and Heine, *Women and Early Christianity,* 28–32.

Women are absent from the images of Christendom, with the exception of Mary. One of the most striking scenes at European cathedrals is the contrast between the beauty of the building and the windows (for instance, at Chartres Cathedral) and the real worshipers, the locals, who cluster around an often tacky-looking doll of Mary.

Chapter 8: The Meeting

Verse: "God our beloved," "Tender God," "Sing out, my soul," and "May the God who shakes heaven and earth" taken from Morley, *All Desires Known,* 69, 77–76, 88. Used by permission. "From the deep places of my soul I praise you, O God" and "Praise be to God, that I have lived to see this day" taken from Jim Cotter's *Prayer at Night's Approaching* (Harrisburg, Pa.: Morehouse Publishing, 1997), 41. Used by permission.

Bibliography

❧

Ashcroft, Mary Ellen. *Balancing Act: How Women Can Lose Their Roles and Find Their Callings.* Downers Grove, Ill.: InterVarsity Press, 1996.

———. *The Magdalene Gospel.* New York: Doubleday, 1995.

Benko, Stephen. *Pagan Rome and the Early Christians.* Bloomington: Indiana University Press, 1984.

Brooten, Bernadette J. *Women Leaders in the Ancient Synagogue: Inscriptional Evidence and Background Issues.* Chico, Calif.: Scholars Press, 1982.

Brown, Raymond E. *The Gospel According to John.* Garden City, N.Y.: Doubleday, 1966.

———. "Roles of Women in the Fourth Gospel." *Theological Studies* 36 (1975): 688–99.

Brox, Norbert. *A Concise History of the Early Church.* New York: Continuum, 1995.

Bruce, F. F. *Paul and Jesus.* Grand Rapids, Mich.: Baker, 1974.

Conzelman, Hans. *History of Primitive Christianity.* Translated by John E. Steely. Nashville: Abingdon, 1973.

Cotter, Jim. *Prayer at Night's Approaching.* Harrisburg, Pa.: Morehouse Publishing, 1991.

Coyle, Kevin. "The Fathers On Women." *Women in Early Christianity,* ed. David M. Scholer. Studies in Early Christianity, vol. 14. New York: Garland, 1993.

Cwiekowski, Frederick J. *The Beginnings of the Church.* New York: Paulist Press, 1988.

D'Angelo, Mary Rose. "Women in Luke—Acts: A Redactional View." *Journal of Biblical Literature* 109 (1990): 441–61.

Dronke, Peter. *Women Writers of the Middle Ages: A Critical Study of Texts from Perpetua to Marguerite Porete.* Cambridge, N.Y.: Cambridge University Press, 1984.

Dunn, James D. G. *Jesus and the Spirit: An inquiry of the Religious and Charismatic Experience of Jesus and the First Christians as Reflected in the New Testament.* London: SCM, 1975.

———. *Jesus, Paul, and the Law: Studies in Mark and Galatians.* Louisville, Ky.: Westminster John Knox, 1990.

———. *Parting of the Ways.* London: SCM, 1991.

———. *Unity and Diversity in the New Testament: An Inquiry into the Character of Earliest Christianity.* Philadelphia: Westminster, 1977.

Evans, Mary. *Woman in the Bible.* London: InterVarsity Press, 1978.

Farris, S. "Hymns in Luke's Infancy Narrative." *Journal for the Study of the New Testament* 9 (October 1985).

Fee, Gordon D. *The First Epistle to the Corinthians.* Grand Rapids, Mich.: Eerdmans, 1987.

Ferguson, Everett. *Backgrounds of Early Christianity.* Grand Rapids, Mich.: Eerdmans, 1993.

———, ed. *Encyclopedia of Early Christianity.* New York: Garland, 1997.

Fiorenza, Elisabeth Schüssler. *In Memory of Her: A Feminist Theological Reconstruction of Christian Origins.* New York: Crossroad, 1994.

Frend, W. H. C. *The Rise of Christianity.* Philadelphia: Fortress Press, 1984.

Giles, K. *Patterns of Ministry among the First Christians.* Melbourne: Collins Dove, 1989.

Glatzer, Nahum. *Hammer on the Rock: A Midrash Reader.* New York: Schocken Books, 1962.

Goodenough, Erwin. "Catacomb Art." *Journal of Biblical Literature*(1962): 113-142.

Grant, Robert M. *Early Christianity and Society: Seven Studies.* San Francisco: Harper and Row, 1977.

Gryson, Roger. *The Ministry of Women in the Early Church.* Translated by Jean Laporte and Mary Louise Hall. Collegeville, Minn.: Liturgical Press, 1976.

Harnack, Adolf von. *The Expansion of Christianity in the First Three Centuries.* New York: G. P. Putnam's Sons, 1904.

Haskins, Susan. *Mary Magdalen: Myth and Metaphor.* New York: Harcourt, Brace and Co., 1993.

Hazlett, Ian, ed. *Early Christianity: Origins and Evolution to A.D. 600.* Nashville: Abingdon, 1991.

Heine, Susanne. *Women and Early Christianity: A Reappraisal.* Translated by John Bowden. Minneapolis: Augsburg Publishing House, 1988.

Hengel, Martin. *Acts and the History of Earliest Christianity.* Translated by John Bowden. Philadelphia: Fortress Press, 1979.

————. *Between Jesus and Paul: Studies in the Earliest History of Christianity.* Translated by John Bowden. Philadelphia: Fortress Press, 1983.

————. *The Charismatic Leader and His Followers.* Translated by James Greig. New York: Crossroad, 1981.

————. *Crucifixion in the Ancient World and the Folly of the Message of the Cross.* Translated by John Bowden. Philadelphia: Fortress Press, 1977.

The Homilies of St. John Chrysostom: Nicene and Post-Nicene Fathers. Grand Rapids, Mich.: Eerdmans, 1956.

Jeremias, Joachim. *Jerusalem in the Time of Jesus: An Investigation into Economic and Social Conditions During the New Testament Period.* Translated by F. H. Cave and C. H. Cave. Philadelphia: Fortress Press, 1969.

Kennedy, George. "Rhetoric of the Early Christian Liturgy," in Jasper, David, and R. C. D. Jasper, *Language and Worship of the Church.* New York: St. Martin's Press, 1990.

Kraemer, Ross Shepard. *Her Share of the Blessings: Women's Religions among Pagans, Jews, and Christians in the Greco-Roman World.* New York: Oxford University Press, 1992.

Kraus, Hans Joachim. *Worship in Israel: A Cultic History of the Old Testament.* Translated by Geoffrey Buswell. Richmond: John Knox, 1966.

Lewis, C. S. *The Allegory of Love: A Study in Medieval Tradition.* Oxford: Clarendon Press, 1936.

MacDonald, Margaret Y. *Early Christian Women and Pagan Opinion: The Power of the Hysterical Woman.* Cambridge, N.Y.: Cambridge University Press, 1996.

Malherbe Abraham. *Social Aspects of Early Christianity.* Baton Rouge: Louisiana State University Press, 1977.

Moltmann-Wendel, Elizabeth. *The Women around Jesus.* Translated by John Bowden. New York: Crossroad, 1982.

Morley, Janet. *All Desires Known.* London: SPCK, 1998.

Murphy-O'Connor, J. (Jerome). *The Holy Land: An Archaeological Guide from Earliest Times to 1700.* 3rd ed. New York: Oxford University Press, 1992.

Neusner, Jacob. *Method and Meaning in Ancient Judaism.* Brown Judaic Studies: Third Series. Missoula, Mont.: Scholars Press, 1979.

———. *What is Midrash?* Philadelphia: Fortress Press, 1987.

Pagels, Elaine. *The Gnostic Gospels.* New York: Random House, 1979.

Perkins, Pheme. *Ministering in the Pauline Churches.* New York: Paulist Press, 1982.

Porton, Gary C. "Defining Midrash." *The Study of Ancient Judaism.* Edited by Jacob Neusner. New York: KTAV, 1981.

Richter Reimer, Ivoni. *Women in the Acts of the Apostles: A Feminist Liberation Perspective.* Translated by Linda M. Maloney. Minneapolis: Fortress Press, 1995.

Sayers, Dorothy L. "The-Human-Not-Quite-Human." *Are Women Human?* Grand Rapids, Mich.: Eerdmans, 1971.

Scholer, David M., ed. *Women in Early Christianity.* Studies in Early Christianity, vol. 14. New York: Garland, 1993.

Schottroff, Luise. *Lydia's Impatient Sisters: A Feminist Social History of Early Christianity.* Louisville, Ky.: Westminster John Knox, 1995.

Schottroff, Luise. "Maria Magdalena und die Frauen am Grabe." Translated by Kirk Allison. *Evangelische Theologie* 42 (1982): 3–35.

Swidler, Leonard. *Biblical Affirmations for Women.* Philadelphia: Westminster, 1977.

Terullianus, Quintus Septimus Florens. *Disciplinary, Moral, and Ascetical Works.* Translated by Rudolph Arbesmann Sr., et al. New York: Fathers of the Church, 1959.

Tetlow, Elizabeth M. *Women and Ministry in the New Testament.* New York: Paulist Press, 1980.

Theissen, Gerd. *Social Reality and the Early Christians: Theology, Ethics, and the World of the New Testament.* Translated by Margaret Kohl. Minneapolis: Fortress Press, 1992.

———. *The Social Setting of Pauline Christianity: Essays on Corinth.* Edited, translated, and with an introduction by John H. Schütz. Philadelphia: Fortress Press, 1982.

———. *Sociology of Early Palestinian Christianity.* Translated by John Bowden. Philadelphia: Fortress Press, 1978.

Thurston, Bonnie Bowman. *The Widows: A Women's Ministry in the Early Church.* Philadelphia: Fortress Press, 1989.

Tyson, Joseph B. *The New Testament and Early Christianity.* New York: Macmillan, 1984.

Warner, Marina. *Alone of All Her Sex: The Myth and the Cult of the Virgin Mary.* New York: Vintage, 1983.

Wolterstorff, Nicholas. *Divine Discourse: Philosophical Reflections on the Claim that God Speaks.* New York: Cambridge University Press, 1995.

Wright, N. T. *Jesus and the Victory of God.* Christian Origins and the Question of God, vol. 2. Minneapolis: Fortress Press, 1996.